W9-AQA-730

SOCCER SKILLS

Way to Play

SOCCER SKILLS

Way to Play

An introductory step-by-step guide

TRIUMPH
BOOKS

Triumph Books and colophon are registered trademarks of Random House, Inc.

This book is available in quantity at special discounts for your group or organization.
For further information, contact:

Triumph Books
542 South Dearborn Street
Suite 750
Chicago, Illinois 60605
(312) 939-3330
Fax (312) 663-3557
www.triumphbooks.com

Printed in Dubai
ISBN: 978-1-60078-630-3

The publishers would like to thank the following sources for their kind permission to
reproduce the pictures in this book.

Allsport UK Ltd: / David Cannon: 68; Getty Images: /Shaun
Botterill/FIFA: 11; /Sebastien Feval/AFP: 20; /Mike Hewitt/FIFA: 3; /Harry How: 18L; /
Karim Jaafar/AFP: 26; /Christof Koepsel/Bongarts: 55; /Pierre-Philippe Marcou/AFP: 44; /
Michael Regan: 51; /Issouf Sanogo/AFP: 30; /Christophe Simon/AFP: 75; /Pedro Ugarte/
AFP: 35, 40; International Sports Images: 18TR, 49; Phil Stevens Photography: 16, 38, 47,
56; Popperfoto: 24, 58, 61; Sporting Pictures (UK) Ltd: 76; Supersport: /Bongarts: 17

Every effort has been made to acknowledge correctly and contact the source and/or
copyright holder of each picture and Carlton Books Limited apologizes for any unintentional
errors or omissions, which will be corrected in future editions of this book.

CONTENTS

INTRODUCTION

Soccer is one of the easiest games to play. It is also the most popular and exciting contact sport in the world with over 117 million players—among them six million women—spread throughout 175 countries. It is watched by billions of fans in stadia and on television throughout the world. The 1994 World Cup, the first finals to be staged in the USA, attracted a world-wide TV audience of 31.5 billion.

"The Beautiful Game," as soccer was once described by Pele, perhaps the greatest player of all time, is also "the people's game." It can be played anywhere and on almost any kind of surface. The great Pele is just one of hundreds of top stars who learned their skills kicking a tennis ball, or tin can, along a beach or backstreet in some remote town or village around the world.

The game gives players the opportunity to combine individual skills with the strength and discipline of teamwork . . . and spectators the thrill and passion of watching players and teams display the different tactics and variety of techniques that make it so special.

This book, *Soccer Skills*, is aimed at providing players of all ages and skill with a better understanding of the game. Even today's great players need to practice and work hard at perfecting their skills. They also need good knowledge of the Laws of the Game to play the game in the right spirit, promote fair play and prove a worthy inspiration to young players hoping to follow in their footsteps.

The first chapter of this book explains in detail the 17 Laws of the Game, including the least understood and most controversial of them all, the offside rule. The second chapter provides hundreds of tips that are of enormous benefit to all young

players. All the game's skills, tactics and techniques are brought to life with full-color illustrations and diagrams, and there are tips on passing, shooting, heading, trapping, dribbling, tackling, plus a special section devoted to goalkeeping. This book also includes an analysis of advanced techniques for experienced players, such as the glancing header, the overhead kick and the swerved pass with the outside of the foot.

The third chapter comprises a study of soccer tactics, including modern-game team formations, offensive and defensive strategies, and set-piece plays, such as corner kicks, free kicks and throw-ins. The book is packed with lots of advice and tips, as well photographs of today's top players in action. Finally, there's a two-page glossary of key soccer terms and an index.

Reading this book and using it to practice the skills and techniques explained in its pages will help you get more satisfaction out of the game and become a better player—whatever skill level you are aiming to achieve.

THE RULES OF THE GAME

To play and enjoy soccer you should be fit and have a good sense of balance, be prepared to practice to improve your skills, and understand the rules. Without a knowledge of the laws of the game neither players nor spectators will never really appreciate the finer points of the game.

The Field of Play

Dimensions

The soccer field is rectangular to ensure the flow of play between the two goals. Its length must not be more than 130 yards (120m) nor less than 100 yards (90m). The width must not be more than 100 yards (90m) or less than 50 yards (45m). The field cannot be square.

The goal area

This is generally known as the "six-yard box" and is formed by measuring six yards (5.5m) from the inside of each goal post along the goal line. Two lines then extend six yards into the Field of Play at right-angles to the goal line. These lines are then connected by a line running parallel to the goal line. The main purpose of the goal area is to indicate where goal kicks should be taken.

The goals

These are the most important pieces of equipment on the Field of Play. They are placed on the center of each goal line and consist of two upright posts, eight yards (7.32m) apart, joined by a horizontal crossbar which must be eight feet (2.44m) from the ground. The width and depth of the goal posts and crossbar must not exceed five inches (12cm). They must be made of wood, metal or other approved material and are white so they can easily be seen.

Nets are attached to the posts and crossbars. They should be properly pegged down at the sides and behind the goal to ensure they don't sag and impede the goalkeeper, or allow the ball to pass underneath.

The Penalty Area

At each end of the field, two lines are drawn at right-angles to the goal line, 18 yards (16.5m) from each goal post. These extend 18 yards into the Field of Play and are joined by a line drawn parallel to the goal line.

This defines the area in which the goalkeeper can handle the ball. A mark is then made within each penalty area 12 yards (11m) from the mid-point of each goal line. This is called the penalty spot. From this spot an arc of a circle

with a radius of ten yards (9.1m) is drawn outside the penalty area. This arc indicates the minimum distance players must be from the ball when a penalty kick is being taken.

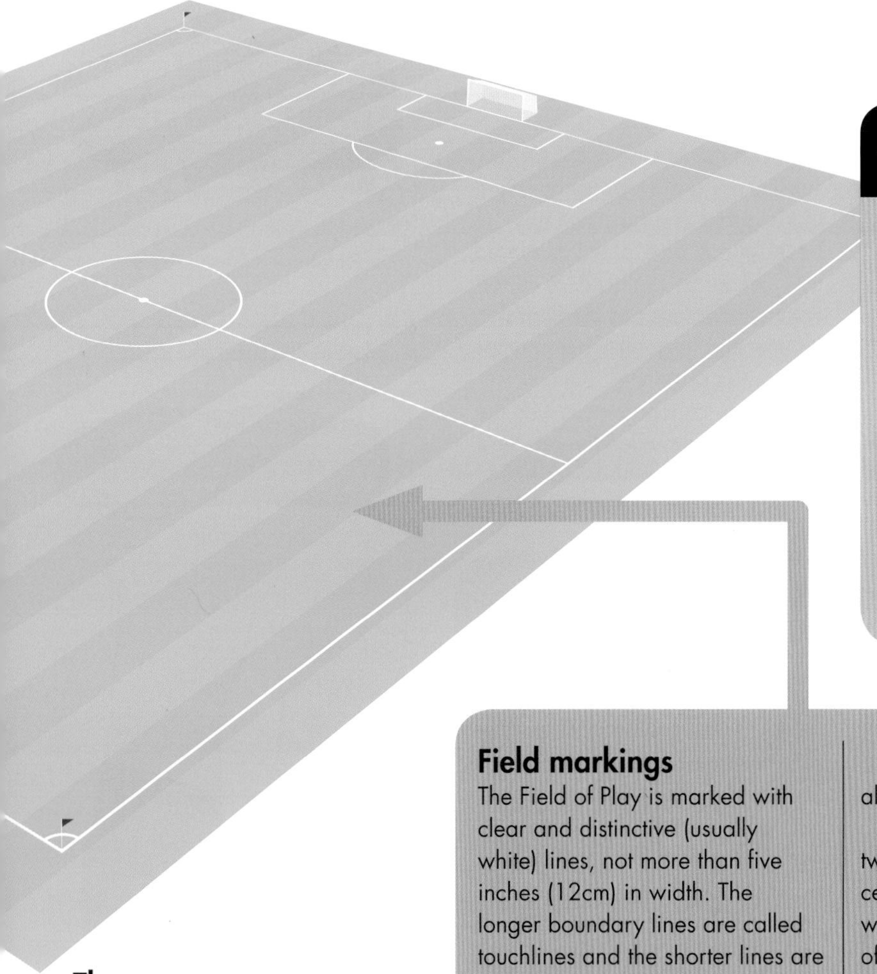

TOP TIPS

CHECK LINES

When you arrive at the ground, always check the field to ensure that all lines are clearly marked. Occasionally, lines may be unclear due to bad weather or because the groundsperson hasn't re-marked the field after the last game. Also check that the lines are not rutted because ruts can cause injury to players who can twist their ankles in them.

The corner area

A small quarter-circle with a one-yard (1m) radius is drawn from each corner flag post inside the Field of Play. This shows the area where the ball must be placed when a corner kick is taken.

Field markings

The Field of Play is marked with clear and distinctive (usually white) lines, not more than five inches (12cm) in width. The longer boundary lines are called touchlines and the shorter lines are the goal lines. Flag posts at least five feet (1.5m) high are placed at each corner of the field. Similar flag posts may be placed at the halfway line, not less than one yard (1m) outside the touchline,

although these are optional.

The Field of Play is divided into two halves by a halfway line. The center of the field is indicated with a suitable mark for the kick-off and a circle with a ten-yard (9.1m) radius is marked around it. This is known as the center circle and enables the referee to ensure the opposing team is standing at least ten yards from the ball at the kick-off.

The ball

The ball must be spherical and made of leather or other approved materials, with a circumference of between 27–28 inches (67.5–70cm) and a weight of 14–16 oz (396–453g). The referee should inspect it before a match to ensure it is neither too hard nor too soft. It should not be changed during a game unless authorized by the referee. Spare balls should always be available.

Number of players

A match is played by two teams, each consisting of 11 players, one of whom must be the goalkeeper. In addition, substitutes, usually three, can be used depending on the rules of the competition. Substitutes can only enter the Field of Play during a stoppage in the game and after they have received a signal from the referee. The substitute must enter the Field of Play at the halfway line, and only after the player being replaced has left the pitch. Once substituted, a player cannot return to the game. If a substitute has been sent off after play has started, they cannot be replaced. In certain competitions, such as the English Premiership, a goalkeeper is among the named substitutes. But any player can change places with the goalkeeper, provided the referee's permission is obtained and the player wears the appropriate jersey.

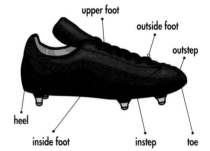

Boots may have cleats or bars for grip that conform to rigid standards to protect other players.

Players' equipment

The soccer uniform, or kit, consists of a shirt (or jersey for goalkeepers), shorts, socks, shinguards and soccer boots. Two types of cleat are used—the molded-sole for hard, dry fields and the screw-in cleated shoe for softer surfaces. The function of cleats, usually made of plastic, rubber, aluminum or other suitable material, is to prevent players from slipping. The advantage of screw-in cleats is that they can be changed to suit the conditions—longer cleats providing better grip on wet and muddy surfaces, and shorter ones more suitable for dry grounds.

Each player on a team must wear the same colored shirts and, to avoid confusion, this color must be different from the opposition's shirts. Goalkeepers must wear distinctively colored jerseys to distinguish them from the outfield players and referee. The goalkeeper may also wear gloves to improve grip on the ball and a cap to keep the sun from the eyes. Numbers are usually displayed on the back of a player's shirt or goalkeeper's jersey.

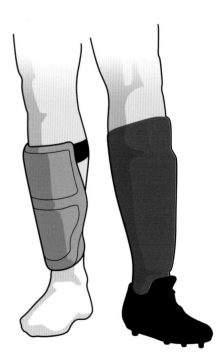

Shinguards must be worn to protect a player's shin.

TOP TIPS

Referees

BALL WORK

Always carry a spare ball, pump and valve adaptors; you'd be surprised how many clubs don't. The referee must check that the match and spare balls are correctly inflated. If a ball is too hard it will bounce excessively, too soft and the ball will be "lifeless" with little bounce, making it difficult to pass accurately.

KEEP BOOTS CLEAN

The most important part of the kit are your boots, so make sure they are comfortable. Boots that are too small can damage your feet, and if they are too big it can be hard to get a good feel of the ball.

A referee is appointed to control the game. The referee's authority and the powers granted under the Laws of the Game take effect immediately on entering the Field of Play. The referee enforces the Laws of the Game; keeps a record of the game; acts as timekeeper and can add on time lost through treatment of injuries or other causes; stops the game at injuries and infringements; can caution or send-off offending players; may suspend or end the game before normal time because of bad weather, trouble caused by spectators, or any other incident that makes such action necessary. The referee's decision on the Field of Play is final and should not be disputed. The referee should wear colors distinctive from the shirts worn by the two opposing teams. No person other than the players and referee's assistant may enter the Field of Play without the referee's permission. A referee should take the following items on to the Field of Play: pencil, notebook, whistle, coin, spare whistle, stopwatch, wristwatch, spare pencil, yellow and red cards.

Referees have to pass an exam which tests their knowledge of the Laws of the Game, and courses are held regularly. Players are encouraged to go on a referee's course so that they get a better understanding of soccer. It is amazing, but many top players do not know all the Laws of the Game.

Once the players and officials enter the Field of Play the referee's word is final.

Referee's assistants

Two referee's assistants are appointed for each match. Their function is to assist the referee in accordance with the Laws. The assistants, one on each touchline, indicate to the referee when the ball is out of play and signal corner kicks, goal kicks or throw-ins.

If an infringement by a player on either team is spotted, the assistant raises a vividly colored flag to attract the referee's attention, who can then decide whether to act on this signal or not. One of the assistant's most important tasks is to signal to the referee when an offensive player strays offside.

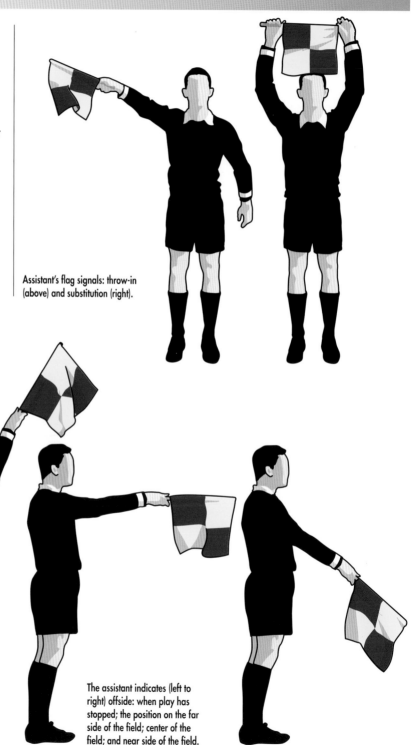

Assistant's flag signals: throw-in (above) and substitution (right).

The assistant indicates (left to right) offside: when play has stopped; the position on the far side of the field; center of the field; and near side of the field.

Game duration

The game is played over two equal periods of 45 minutes (known as halves), unless otherwise agreed upon by the two teams. Any time lost through injury, time-wasting or substitutions can be added on at the referee's discretion. Extra time is also allowed for a player to take a penalty kick if one is awarded at, or after, the end of normal time in either half. The half-time interval should not exceed 15 minutes except by consent of the referee. However, it is common to have half-time intervals of more extended periods at some televised matches.

The start of play

To start a game, the two captains toss a coin for choice of ends, or the right to kick-off. Before the kick-off, the referee should ensure the ball is stationary on the center spot.

Opponents must not come into the center circle—within ten yards (9.1m) of the ball—until the ball has been kicked. On the referee's whistle, the game is started by a player kicking the ball forwards.

Once played, the ball must travel its own circumference before being touched by another player. The player kicking-off must not play the ball again until it has been touched by another player. The game should be restarted in the same manner, although at the start of the second half the teams should change ends. The team which didn't kick-off in the first half has the second-half kick-off.

Ball in and out of play

The ball is out of play when (a) the whole of the ball has crossed the goal or touchlines, either on the ground or in the air and (b) when the game has been stopped by the referee. The ball is in play at all other times, including when it rebounds off the goal posts, corner flags or the referee.

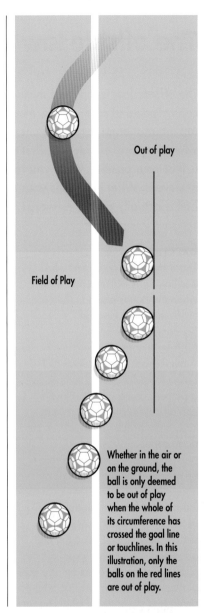

Out of play

Field of Play

Whether in the air or on the ground, the ball is only deemed to be out of play when the whole of its circumference has crossed the goal line or touchlines. In this illustration, only the balls on the red lines are out of play.

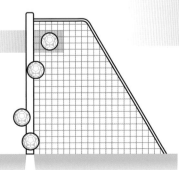

In this illustration, only the ball in the pale blue area at the top counts as having crossed the goal line. If the goalkeeper were to stop any of the others at their current positions, the goal will have been saved.

Scoring

A goal is scored when the whole of the ball crosses the goal line, either on the ground or in the air, between the goal posts and under the cross-bar. The team scoring the most goals wins the game. If the number of goals scored is equal the result is a draw.

The offside law

The offside law is the most misunderstood and controversial of all the rules. Many players, even top internationals, are often unaware exactly when they are offside. The first thing to remember is that your position when you receive the ball is irrelevant. What matters is your position when the ball is actually played forwards. If, at the moment the ball is passed, there are fewer than two defenders between an offensive player and the goal, the offensive player is offside—remember the goalkeeper usually counts as one of the two defenders. When you are attacking, if you are level with the last defender with only the goalkeeper in front of you, you are not offside.

Exceptions

There are three occasions when positioning is not relevant, even when the ball is played. They are:
(1) from a goal kick; or
(2) from a throw-in; or
(3) from a corner kick.

But in each case as soon as the ball is touched by a teammate, a player can be offside. Players can also be offside from a free kick, a drop-kick or throw from the goalkeeper.

An offensive player can also be offside if the ball bounces off a teammate and goes forwards to the attacker, even if an opposing defender is the last player to deliberately kick or head the ball. If a teammate's forward pass touches a defender and goes to an offensive player in an offside position with no defenders closer to the goal line, the player is still offside.

Other times when an offensive player is not offside with no defenders closer to the goal line, are when the ball is passed backwards by a teammate who is closer to goal (however, when the receiving player shoots, the teammate may be offside), or if a player is in their own half of the field when the ball is played. The new rule states that a player shall not be declared offside

Below and opposite: three examples of onside and offside positions. Dotted lines represent the path of the ball, red lines the movement of players. Attackers are in red shorts, defenders in blue shirts and white shorts. The goalkeeper is in green.

Player (A) is offside because there is only one defender (the goalkeeper) between them and the goal when the ball is played.

unless, when in an offside position, they make an active attempt to play the ball. This means players can now stand anywhere on the field as long as they are not in line with the goalkeeper without being offside. Only when a teammate passes the ball to them, or they deliberately run towards the ball will they be declared offside.

Interfering with play

At this point, it is worth thinking about the phrase, "not interfering with play." Usually, this only happens when the ball is crossed backwards from the wings. At a corner, for instance, the corner taker may be closer to the goal line than any defender, but is clearly not interfering with play.

Player (A) is offside because although Player (X) is closer to the goal, the goalkeeper (Y) and Player (Z) are actually in front of Player (A), so there is only one defender between the offensive player and the goal.

If you realize that you are in an offside position as an offensive move develops, you may be tempted to step off the field to indicate non-interference with play. But this will result in a caution from the referee for leaving the field without permission.

If you get injured, the referee or their assistant may consider you to be "not interfering with play," but if you then get up and run after the ball, you may be declared offside.

Free kick

The referee will award an indirect free kick to the opposing team if a player is declared offside. This is taken from the spot where the infringement occurred, unless the offense is committed by a player in the opponents' goal area. In this case, the free kick should be taken from any point within the goal area.

Player (A) is onside. Although only the goalkeeper is closer to the goal line than the front two offensive players, because Player (B) has run past two defenders (from B1–B2), the cross has been pulled back to Player (A).

Offside trap

This tactic is often used by defenders to force offensive players deliberately offside. While marking the offensive players as they wait for a pass, the defenders suddenly move out in a line as the ball is about to be played, leaving the offensive players stranded in an offside position.

Using this tactic successfully requires good teamwork and discipline. Used properly, it is an effective method of frustrating attacks. But defenders should not get complacent since the trap can be beaten by an offensive player dribbling the ball through the defensive line, or a quick passing movement.

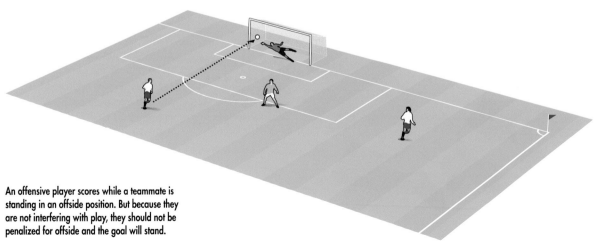

An offensive player scores while a teammate is standing in an offside position. But because they are not interfering with play, they should not be penalized for offside and the goal will stand.

Fouls and misconduct

Law 12 was not devised to discourage the physical effort needed to play the game. It provides a code of discipline to enable you to display your skills in a physical contact game by protecting you against unnecessary force and foul play. Law 12 comprises three parts: (a) major offenses, (b) other offenses and (c) misconduct.

The major offenses

There are nine major, or penal offenses which, if committed intentionally, are penalized by awarding a direct free kick to the opposing team. Eight of the nine offenses are concerned with physical foul play against opponents. Should a defending player intentionally commit any of these nine offenses within the penalty area, a penalty kick will be awarded.

The penal offenses are:

(1) Kicking, or attempting to kick an opponent;
(2) Tripping an opponent using the legs or stooping in front of, or behind, an opponent;
(3) Jumping at an opponent;
(4) Charging in a violent or dangerous manner;
(5) Charging an opponent from behind in a violent or dangerous manner (unless the opponent is guilty of obstruction);
(6) Striking, attempting to strike, or spitting at an opponent;
(7) Holding an opponent with the hand or arm;
(8) Pushing an opponent;
(9) Handling the ball with any part of the hand or arm.

Other non-penal offenses

Offenses penalized with an indirect free kick are:

(1) Dangerous play (attempting to kick the ball while held by the goalkeeper, attempting to kick a ball close to the head of an opponent);

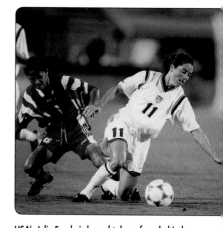

USA's Julie Foudy is brought down from behind.

(2) Charging an opponent fairly, but while not attempting to play the ball (shoulder charging an opponent fairly, but when the ball is not within playing distance);
(3) Obstruction (blocking an opponent's path to the ball when it is not within playing distance);
(4) Charging the goalkeeper (unless they are holding the ball, obstructing an opponent, or have gone outside the goal area);
(5) Goalkeeper not releasing the ball into play properly (when more than four steps are taken while holding, bouncing or throwing the ball in the air before releasing it. After releasing the ball, the goalkeeper is not allowed to touch it again with the hands until it has been played by

Whether intentional or not, tripping up an opponent is foul play. Here the culprit is clearly not aiming for the ball in the tackle.

another player. The goalkeeper is, however, permitted to play the ball with their feet);

(6) Time-wasting by the goalkeeper (if the referee considers the ball is held for an unreasonable time, or the goalkeeper indulges in other tactics considered by the referee to be wasting time to unfairly give advantage to their own team);

(7) If a teammate deliberately passes with the foot to the goalkeeper and the keeper uses a hand or hands to control the ball. A good referee will let the keepers know if they can handle a sliced clearance, or tackle.

The "professional foul"

If you are denied an obvious goal-scoring opportunity by an opponent deliberately handling the ball, or by unfairly impeding your path to goal, it is classed as serious foul play and the referee should dismiss the offender from the Field of Play.

Dangerous play, such as kicking at a high ball in another player's face, is an offense which will be penalized.

Misconduct

To avoid committing offenses, all players should understand the Laws of the Game, accept the referee's decisions without argument, and conduct themselves as sportsmen and sportswomen. Referees will caution you by showing the yellow card, and award an indirect free kick to the opposing team, if you:

(1) enter, or reenter the Field of Play after the game has started, or leave the Field of Play during the game (except through accident), without first gaining permission from the referee;

(2) show by word or action, dissent from any refereeing decision;

(3) are guilty of unsporting conduct;

(4) persistently infringe the Laws of the Game.

The referee will show you the red card and send you off if you are guilty of:

(1) violent conduct, or serious foul play;

(2) using foul and abusive language;

(3) a second yellow card offense after previously receiving a caution.

The referee signals an indirect free kick. These are awarded for obstruction, dissent or unsporting conduct.

If the referee stops play to dismiss a player without that player having committed a foul (for example, the player might have sworn at the assistant or left the field without permission) the game will resume with an indirect free kick to the opposing team from the place where the infringement took place.

TOP TIPS

UNSPORTING CONDUCT
Often a player will shout "My ball!" or "Leave it!" when going for the ball. Opponents can be distracted by this and hesitate when making a challenge for the ball. If you do shout, always use a player's name, for example: "Gill King's ball!" or "Goalkeeper's ball!" Holding an opponent back by their shirt, or climbing on their back to gain extra height are two other examples of unfair play. Above all, remember a referee's decision is final—don't argue with referee or assistant, or you could get booked for dissent.

Free kicks

A free kick can be either direct or indirect and is always taken from the spot where the offense occurred (except for a penalty kick, below). The ball must be stationary when the kick is taken and it must be touched by another player before the kicker is allowed to strike it again. While a player can score from a direct free kick, a goal cannot be scored from an indirect free kick until the ball has been touched by another player. To indicate that a free kick is indirect the referee will raise one arm above their head.

When defending a free kick, players must be at least ten yards (9.1m) from the ball, except when

The referee clearly indicates that a free kick has been awarded.

an indirect free kick has been awarded less than ten yards from the goal. Opponents may then stand between the goal posts or on the goal line.

If the defending team is awarded a free kick in its own penalty area, the ball must be kicked out of the area and no opponents may enter the area until the kick is taken.

Direct free kicks around the opposition's goal area can be a great opportunity to score.

The penalty kick

A penalty kick often proves crucial in a match.

A penalty—a free shot on goal taken from the penalty spot—is awarded if the defending team commits a foul inside its own penalty area that would normally be punished by a direct free kick. All players, with the exception of the goalkeeper and the player taking the kick, must stand outside the penalty area, at least ten yards (9.15m) from the penalty spot.

There are three basic rules regarding penalty kicks:

(1) the goalkeeper must stand on the goal line until the ball is kicked (though they may move from side to side);
(2) the player taking the kick must kick the ball forwards;
(3) the penalty-taker must not touch the ball a second time until it has been touched by another player.

As penalty kicks are a vital part of the game, time can be extended at half time or full time to allow them to be taken, or retaken. There are only three reasons why a kick

should be retaken; these are if:
(1) the defending team breaks the law and a goal is not scored;
(2) the attacking team, with the exception of the kicker, infringes and a goal is scored;
(3) there are infringements by players of both teams. If the kicker breaks the law (by playing the ball twice for example) the defending team is awarded an indirect free kick.

Throw-in

Originally designed as a means of getting the ball back into play as quickly as possible, the throw-in has developed into an effective offensive technique. Some players have developed a "long throw," that is almost as effective as a corner kick if it is awarded close to the opponent's penalty area.

The throw-in should be taken on the touchline at the point where the ball went out of play, and the ball must be thrown into play with both hands, from behind and over the head. The thrower must face the Field of Play and, as the ball is released, part of each foot must be on the ground on, or behind, the touchline.

If these rules are broken, or the thrower attempts to gain an unfair advantage by moving along the touchline, the throw-in will be given to the opposing team.

A goal cannot be scored direct from a throw-in, and the thrower may not touch the ball again until it has been touched by another player.

For the throw-in, the throwing player must have both feet on or behind the touchline, and at least a part of both feet must remain in contact with the ground during the throw. Both hands, placed either side of the ball (or behind it in the case of a long throw, see pages 42–43), must be used for the throw-in.

Goal kick

Goal kicks (kicks taken from within the goal area returning the ball into play) are awarded to the defending team when the ball crosses its goal line, outside the goal, after having last been touched by an opponent.

Although goalkeepers generally take goal kicks, they may be taken by any other player. When taking a goal kick the ball must travel outside the penalty area, although a "short goal kick" (a pass to a defender standing just outside the penalty-area) is a good way of retaining possession and setting up an attack.

A long goal kick can be very effective, because offensive players cannot be offside from a goal kick. A goal cannot be scored direct from a goal kick, and if this happens the game is restarted with a goal kick to the opposing team.

Corner kick

A corner kick is awarded to the offensive team if the ball crosses the goal line, either in the air or on the ground, having last been played by one of the defending team. It is taken from the quarter-circle by the corner flag on the appropriate side of the field. The flag must not be removed to take the kick, and opponents must stand at least ten yards (9.1m) away from the ball until it is in play. As with a free kick, the kicker must not play the ball again until it has been touched by another player, although unlike an indirect free kick, a goal can be scored direct from a corner kick.

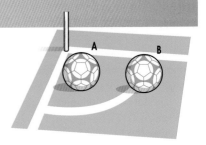

The corner kick must be taken from within the quarter-circle, so the ball at position B will not be allowed.

SKILLS AND TECHNIQUES

To be a soccer success, you need a combination of natural skill and dedication to improve constantly your techniques. You need to master the basic skills of the game, and must be able to control the ball, pass it to a teammate, shoot with either foot, head the ball and tackle opponents when necessary—in fact, develop a good balance of skills relating to the position you play. You will also need the vision to read games and playing situations. One thing's for sure, no matter if you are an international star, or whether you play for fun, you can never learn enough about the game.

Kicking the ball

Being able to kick the ball correctly is the most important basic skill in the game to master. You need total control of the ball to ensure it goes where you want it to at the right pace.

Any part of the foot can be used to kick the ball, although you should avoid kicking with your toes, because control is more difficult with this part of the foot.

Most players can kick a stationary ball quite easily, but you need to concentrate and to practice all the different kicking techniques to be able to take corner kicks, free kicks and to pass, cross and shoot properly during match-play action.

Kicking the ball correctly is the most important soccer skill to master. Players should learn to keep their head down and eyes over the ball.

The pass with inside of the foot

The inside of your foot is the area from your heel to big toe. This kicking area is used for short, accurate, low passes of up to 20 yards (18m). This is the easiest way of passing the ball to a teammate because such a large area of foot is used for the kick, therefore eliminating the room for error.

To make the pass, place the non-kicking foot alongside the ball and point it in the direction you wish to send the ball, keeping your head down and eyes over it as you pre-pare to kick. Now, raise your kicking foot two to three inches (5–8cm) off the ground, turning it out almost at right-angles. Keeping the ankle firm, bring your foot back and strike the ball firmly in its center. Finally, follow through with your kicking foot to guide the ball in the intended direction.

There are many examples of ex-emplary passers of the ball, such as Brazil's Kaka and Landon Donovan of the USA. Both are superb pass-masters of the ball; whether they are looking to find a teammate over a short distance or a long one.

The pass with outside of the foot

The outside of the foot is the flat area from the ankle to the end of the toes. It's difficult to kick the ball straight using this area, so it is used—mainly by experienced players—to curl, or bend the ball in flight. The knee and kicking foot are turned inwards and the outside front of the foot makes contact with the ball. Raise the kicking foot off the ground slightly and strike the center of the ball. This skill is useful when faced with an opponent moving in to challenge you—flick the ball away to one side to a teammate, or bend it around the challenger.

Kicking the ball with the outside of the foot is perfect for swerving passes or shots.

To ensure a powerful and accurate lofted kick use the instep of the foot, strike beneath the ball and use a full follow-through.

The lofted kick

The instep of the foot is used for long-distance passes over the heads of opponents, crossing the ball into the area or corner kicks. To make the kick, lean backwards with the supporting foot to the side of and slightly behind the ball. Once in position, strike beneath the ball to give you the necessary lift and follow through with a full leg swing.

SOCCER PRACTICE

- A good way to improve your accuracy is to kick a ball against a wall that has been marked with numbered targets. Start by aiming for target box 1. If you hit it, go for box 2 and so on. You can practice this on your own or with several players. When you miss the target, it is another player's turn. Every time it's your turn, aim for the target you missed last time. As your accuracy improves, move further away from the target and shoot from different angles.

- Set up two cones (or similar objects) a small distance apart. Aim to kick the ball between the cones to a friend, who kicks the ball back.

- Split your team into two lines on either side of a goal. Have one player from each group throw the ball at varying angles for each player in turn to trap and then kick towards goal.

- Stand between two players who are about 30 yards (27m) apart. As they lob the ball over your head, attempt to head it away. If you're successful, change places with one of the kickers. As your heading ability improves, try using two soccer balls.

- In a marked area, players at each end bend the ball around a defender who is positioned in the middle.

The chip shot

If performed correctly, this is one of the most dangerously rewarding offensive kicks in the game. The chip shot can be used to score goals by lifting the ball over the head of the goalkeeper who has strayed too far off the goal line, open up the tightest of defenses to put a teammate in a good offensive position and to clear your lines if under pressure. To play a chip shot place the kicking foot and instep under the ball and flick your ankle. To make the ball rise steeply, there should always be a short leg backlift and very little follow-through.

The half-volley requires the same concentration and judgment as the volley, but the ball is struck after hitting the ground. Again, the instep should be the striking area to ensure power and to control the low trajectory.

The volley: note how the player swivels on the non-kicking foot and uses the instep of the other foot to strike the ball. Fine judgment of the ball's flight and pace is essential. The kick is made before the ball hits the ground.

With a stabbing movement, strike the ball on its underside for the chip shot. A ball rolling towards you is easier to chip accurately than a stationary one.

The volley and half-volley

One of soccer's most spectacular sights is a goal scored from a long-range volley. Spain's Fernando Torres practices volleying the ball every day during training, and has delighted fans with many stunning goals scored this way. Timing and concentration are vital for accuracy, and for maximum power the instep should be used to strike the ball.

Keep your eyes firmly on the ball when preparing for a volley, and try to judge the ball's line of flight and pace. Leaning back away from the ball, balance on the non-kicking foot, swivel your body and strike the ball before it hits the ground— pointing the toes downwards helps give extra power. Once contact

is made, follow through with the kicking leg.

The half-volley is when you kick the ball just after it has hit the ground. Like the volley, the half-volley requires full concentration and good judgment to predict the ball's flight.

To kick a ball on the half-volley, place your non-kicking foot close to the spot where you estimate the ball is going to bounce. As it hits the ground, swing your kicking foot to make contact with the bouncing ball using the instep. Be sure to follow through the ball, keeping the kicking foot pointing down and forwards to give the ball a low trajectory and maximize the shot's power.

Unorthodox kicks

Overhead kicks, also known as bicycle kicks, can be used to catch goalkeepers by surprise, or to get a player out of trouble in defense. If the kick comes off and a spectacular goal is scored, you are a hero. If it doesn't you can be left flat on your back, out of the action and looking like a clown.

As the ball comes over, your kicking foot should be at full stretch, with your toes reaching for it. Impact with the ball should be made with the flat of the foot on the cleatlace area, with the toes pointed towards your instep. Bend the knee

of the non-kicking leg to ensure your body leans backwards. Bend your elbows and spread your hands to break your fall.

A swerving or curved pass can be used to make an inswinging corner kick, or to swerve the ball around a defensive wall. The inside or outside of the foot may be used to curve the ball. Striking the ball's left side curves it to the right, and striking its right side curves it to the left. Leaning your body over the ball helps you gain greater control.

The bicycle kick is certainly the most visually exciting of the unorthodox kicks, requiring almost a somersault. Make sure that your elbows are bent and hands outstretched to break your fall.

INSET: the back-heel kick can be used to deceive opponents. Step over the ball you are dribbling, stop suddenly and use the heel to kick the ball back to a teammate in position.

The back-heel

This technique can be used effectively to wrong-foot opponents. For example, you can deceive an opponent by shaping to dribble the ball past the challenger then suddenly stopping, stepping over the ball and back-heeling it to a teammate, leaving your opponent stranded. A word of caution, though; never attempt a back-heel in front of your own goal.

When performing a back-heel, the supporting leg should be close to the ball. For power and accuracy, always try to strike the middle of the ball with the back of the heel. A slower but more accurate method of back-heeling is to use the sole of the boot to stop the ball before making contact. Only use this method if you have plenty of time.

Shooting

The aim of all soccer matches is to score more goals than your opponents. Quality goalscorers are essential to every team, that's why strikers such as Argentina's Carlos Tevez, who is considered to be the best striker in the world, are amongst soccer's most wanted players.

Although the goalscorer usually gets all the praise, the build-up to a goal requires team-work, keeping possession of the ball, building an offense and opening defenses to create space in front of goal for the strikers to finish.

Many strikers are natural, goal-hungry predators who rely on pure instinct—nothing is more important to them than seeing the back of the net bulge.

Confidence, pace, height, control and body strength are a striker's vital assets. A striker also needs to be brave to stand the knocks that occur in the penalty area. Germany's Birgit Prince and Abby Wambach of the USA are classic examples of the all-round, all-action striker. They have the ability to use all their skills and power while under pressure.

As a goalscorer you need a sixth sense of where the goal is so you can shoot from any angle or distance without looking up. If you hesitate on the ball, even for a split-second, a good scoring chance is often lost.

The golden rule of shooting is always to hit the target and force the goalkeeper into making a save. Shots on goal need power and accuracy if they are to beat the goalkeeper, but don't always rely on pure force, because even the fiercest of shots can be saved by a goalkeeper's outstretched leg, arm or foot. Remember, a goalkeeper also has instincts . . . for stopping the ball.

Goals can be scored with a number of different kicks, including gentle taps, chips, volleys or curling shots around the goalkeeper. These techniques and skills have been covered on pages 20–23.

Goals can also be scored by putting pressure on defenders and goalkeepers in the penalty area and seizing any opportunity to stab the ball into the net.

Basic techniques

Your team may create many goalscoring opportunities in a game, but fail to take advantage of any of them and you may lose. To ensure you grab as many chances as possible you must simulate match conditions in practice by shooting with moving balls.

Shooting covers several kicking and passing techniques that have been explained on pages 20–23. The art of good shooting is to strike a balance between control, accuracy and power—and to be able to kick with both feet!

Balance, control, accuracy and power—the perfect shooting technique. Practicing your shooting regularly will help ensure you make the most of goal scoring opportunities in match situations.

When shooting, position your supporting foot alongside the ball with toes pointing in the direction you want it to go. With eyes firmly on the ball, keep your head and shoulders over the ball, using your arms for balance. Swing back the kicking leg with toes pointed outwards and then strike the ball in the middle with your instep. The kicking knee should be over the ball at the moment of impact to keep the shot low. With your head down and toes tensed and pointed, follow through with the kicking leg, adding power from the knee. If the ball has been struck with great power the force should lift your body off the ground.

If the ball is moving away from you as you are about to shoot, place your kicking foot ahead of it and strike with your toes pointed and tensed.

Shooting from a distance

You need to be able to kick with great power and be aware of the situation around you to shoot from long range. Always consider passing the ball to a teammate who is in a better position to score than you are. Also be aware of the goalkeeper's position—a surprise shot from outside the area could catch them and the opposing defenders off guard.

For maximum power, the non-kicking foot should be alongside

SOCCER PRACTICE

- Use a wall to practice shooting and ball control. Mark out targets and use both feet when kicking. Start by standing four to five yards from the wall, gradually increasing the distance between you and the wall. See how many times you can hit the target in a minute.

- Get two players to stand on either side of the penalty area and take it in turns to fire balls towards the penalty spot at all angles and heights for a third player to run on to and kick while they are moving. If no goalkeeper is available, shoot at a wall.

- During five-a-side games or training, try occasionally not to use your good foot. If you are naturally right-footed, play the ball with your left. Or play with a cleat on your weak foot and a softer training shoe on your strong foot.

- Practice volleying by getting a friend to throw the ball towards the penalty spot for you to strike before it hits the ground. When you have improved get another player to act as a defender and run from behind you and try to get the ball before you can kick it. This gets you used to being under pressure and helps speed up your reactions.

- For chip shots, place a number of balls on the edge of the penalty area and see how many times you can hit the crossbar with them.

For a long-distance shot make sure the non-kicking foot is alongside the ball. Use the arms for balance and kick with the top of the foot, and then follow through.

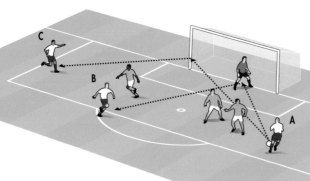

Player (A) shoots for a goal. If the shot is pushed out by the goalkeeper or strikes the far post the ball could rebound to Player (B) or Player (C).

Power, poise and accuracy are essential for good shooting. These, plus anticipation and pure instinct, are traits of a top-class striker.

the ball with your head over the ball. Arms should be outstretched to the side for balance. The ball should be struck with the top of the foot not with the toes—keep them down. Remember, keep your eyes on the ball and follow through with the kicking leg after making contact with the ball.

Your head must be down over the ball in order to keep the shot close to the ground. Low shots, particularly when aimed at the corners of the goal, are more difficult for the goalkeeper to deal with than a high shot directed just under the crossbar.

England's David Beckham is famous for his long-range shooting and has scored many important goals.

Another long-range expert is the USA's Kristine Lilly.

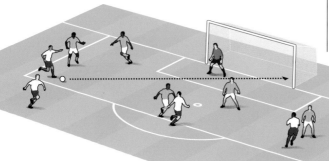

When shooting from the edge of the penalty area, always aim just inside the far post.

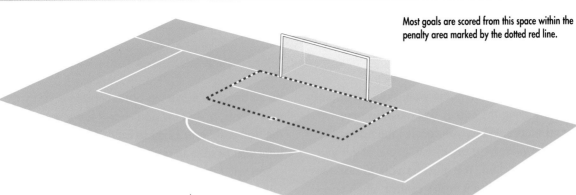

Most goals are scored from this space within the penalty area marked by the dotted red line.

Shooting from close range

Top-class strikers like Uruguay's Luis Suárez score many goals by pure instinct and reflex action from inside the six-yard (5.5m) box. Anticipation and accuracy are more important than power in close-range situations. Always be on the look-out for rebounds, stay alert and be ready to pounce on the loose ball and gently tap, or side-foot the ball into the net.

Positioning in the penalty area

Most goals are scored from an area that extends from the goal line to the penalty spot (above). The best area for scoring goals is seen by drawing a line from the goal posts to the edge of the penalty area, as shown in the diagram below. Inside the blue area you should pass the ball to a teammate who might be better positioned. Inside the red area shoot for goal!

While play is inside the penalty area, be aware of what's happening around you and get into a position to snap up balls that have rebounded off posts, defenders' legs, or been parried by the goalkeeper. However, don't get caught offside! If a shot misses the target and flies across the goal, a player running in at the far post will have a good chance of reaching the ball and scoring.

TOP TIPS

EYES ON THE BALL
It's important to keep your eyes firmly on the ball when making contact with it. Before you strike the ball, look to see where the goalkeeper is. You can take advantage of a badly positioned goalkeeper.

DON'T BE AFRAID TO MISS
When shooting from long range don't be afraid of missing. If you are nervous you will lack confidence, which will probably affect your accuracy.

Don't always aim for the center of the goal. Pick a target such as the far post, or corner of the goal—vulnerable spots for goalkeepers.

Always follow up shots and make sure the ball has crossed the line if you are in any doubt.

Never change your mind as you prepare to shoot. The player who hesitates loses.

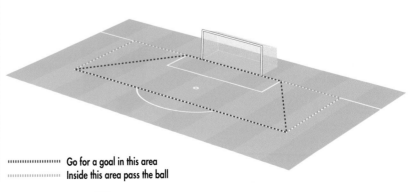

.... Go for a goal in this area
.... Inside this area pass the ball

Trapping the ball

If you are to play the game well, skilled trapping and controlling the soccer ball must become second nature. When you receive the ball your first touch must be a good one, especially if you are tightly marked. You must be able to stop the ball dead and bring it under control, often under pressure in a crowded area of the field.

A good first touch gives you space and time to make the next move—a pass, negotiate opponents, a shot for goal—or it lets you shield the ball with your body to hold off a challenge until you're able to make a positive move.

You will become an accomplished team player with mastery of ball control. Without, opposing players will find it easy to mark you tightly, giving them the initiative to take the ball from you.

Basic technique

Whichever part of the body is used to control or trap the ball the basic technique is the same. Keep your eyes firmly on the ball and get your body into the line of flight, so you are perfectly balanced and ready to take it in your stride. At the moment of impact, relax the part of the body you are using to control the ball. This movement acts as a cushion and slows down the ball, making it easier to control, whereas a rigid leg, foot, chest or head acts as a firm barrier off which the ball will bounce away from you.

Be positive and aware of how you're going to trap the ball and position your body accordingly, especially if you're being tightly marked by an opponent.

Trapping the ball with the inside of the foot

Keep your eyes on the ball, with your balancing foot firmly on the ground. Use the raised foot making contact with the ball to absorb, or cushion, its power by pulling the foot back slightly at the moment of impact. The ball should drop to the ground after hitting the leg, making it easy to control with the inside of your foot. You are then ready to

move away with the ball, or pass to a teammate.

The trapping foot should be relaxed to cushion the ball. The

Trapping the ball with the inside of the foot (top) and the outside (bottom).

more pace you can take off the ball, the easier it is to control. Keep your balance so that you can move quickly away with the ball. Timing is also important, or the ball could bounce away from you.

Trapping the ball with the outside of the foot

To trap the ball with the outside of your foot, lean your body towards the ball's flight. At the moment of impact the foot should be relaxed and the knee slightly bent to cushion and slow down the ball's pace. If you are about to be challenged, keep your supporting leg between the ball and your opponent. This helps to retain your balance and shield the ball from a challenger. You should now be ideally placed to pass to a teammate, or go around an opponent. If you are being marked, your opponent will find it difficult to tackle and get the ball from you without committing a foul.

Chest traps

When a high ball is falling, a player may not be able to wait for it to reach the ground before trapping and getting it under control. In this situation the chest trap is the answer. Often high balls crossed into the penalty area have to be controlled at chest height before a striker is in a position to shoot for goal. An experienced defender also deflects balls away from danger by turning the chest as the ball hits it, but you should always try to head the ball clear.

To perform the chest trap you must keep your eyes on the ball, get your body in line with its flight as it comes towards you, and correct your balance by using your arms. Watching the ball closely as it continues to drop, bend your knees slightly and extend your arms. You should be on your toes and leaning back slightly as the ball makes contact with your chest. Try to cushion the impact by relaxing your chest muscles and lean your head over the ball as it falls to your feet. Great defenders such as England's John Terry and Italy's Fabio Cannavaro have perfected the chest trap and often use it to deflect the ball to safety. In all-round play they have contributed hugely towards the

In a chest trap, the ball's impact is cushioned by leaning back and relaxing the chest muscles to bring the ball under control.

If the ball is falling towards you at an awkward angle, use the thigh trap to stop it and bring it under control.

TOP TIPS

CUSHION CONTROL
You can gain control of the ball more quickly and more effectively by taking the pace off it. As the ball hits your legs or chest, relax the muscles, bending your legs slightly on impact to cushion it.

ONE TOUCH
Remember to control the ball with your first touch, and to pass or to take opponents on or shoot for goal with your second. This way you don't give opponents the opportunity to tackle you.

defensive strength of their respective teams through clearing the imminent danger on several occasions by pushing the ball away with their chest. They do this by tensing their chest at the moment of impact and twisting their body from the hips to send the ball in the direction they want.

Thigh traps
The thigh is often used to control a ball that's dropping towards you at an awkward height when you're on the move. It can also be used to push the ball into the air to allow you to volley it with the other leg. The thigh control makes the ball drop to the feet quicker than the chest trap. Turn your body towards the ball, relax the thigh muscles and allow it to hit your thigh. Ensuring your supporting leg is slightly bent, let the ball drop to your feet, leaving you ready to pass, or quickly turn and lose your marker.

SOCCER PRACTICE

- Make a triangle using three players. Trap and pass the ball between you. Keep the ball moving and pass over longer distances as you improve your control.

- A simple solo exercise is to throw a ball into the air and trap it as it falls to the ground, using the inside of your foot.

- One player passes to you when you're positioned inside the center circle. Trap the ball while being challenged by a third player and try to pass back to the first player, who runs around the edge of the center circle. Take it in turns to change position.

- Find two walls at right-angles. Kick the ball against one wall and when it comes back trap and hit it against the other wall. Use your feet and head in five- to ten-minute spells. Increase the times as you improve.

Running with the ball

One of the most exciting sights in the game is to see a player go on a run and dribble the ball past several opponents, while keeping it under close control. The player weaves one way then the other, evading tackle after tackle before using the developed pace to leave opponents stranded.

Brazil's Kaka possesses all the attributes of a superb attacking player and is a prime example for all young players to watch and to try to emulate.

Always remember, though, soccer is a team game; dribbling past three or four defenders and then losing the ball to a fifth who starts a dangerous counter-attack is no good to your team. Dribbling and running with the ball are

The best dribblers use balance and control to run with the ball.

most effective on the wings, especially against tight defenses.

Once near the goal line you can cross the ball to teammates positioned in front of the goal. Defenders forced into a tackle are often left stranded, or have to concede a corner.

To have good dribbling skills you need ball control, balance, pace, and quick reactions in one-on-one situations.

Running with the ball to get away from opponents and move into space requires pace, close control and an awareness of the players around you. When you're running with the ball look around to spot opponents who appear set to challenge you, or teammates who are in good positions to receive your pass.

Basic techniques

When dribbling a ball, think of it as part of your foot. Lean over the ball and keep it within comfortable distance, close enough to control but with space to let you move away, or change direction if you are challenged. Look to see how your opponent is standing. If they are flat-footed, instead of on their toes, they will be slow off the mark when challenging or chasing you.

When running with the ball, push it slightly ahead. The faster you run the further you can push the ball. Try to combine pace and balance

with a body-swerve and a dip of the shoulder to confuse your opponent about your intended direction.

Keeping the ball on the blind side

When you're in possession of the ball and are being closely marked you may have to move forward, or (more often than not) keep the ball until you're in a better position to release it. Protect or shield the ball from an opponent by keeping your body between the two, preventing your opponent from seeing, or reaching the ball.

With your head leaning forwards, put your weight on the non-kicking foot. Hold your arms out slightly behind your body. This helps your balance and makes it difficult for your opponent to tackle.

Run with the ball as the opponent moves in to tackle from the side. As you're challenged from the left, control the ball with the outside of your right foot, or the outside of your left foot if challenged from the right.

Twist and turn your back to your opponent and use a body-swerve, or dummy to move away with the ball on the opponent's blind side.

Change of pace

Move towards an opponent at your normal speed but when you close, drop a shoulder and veer away, slightly stepping up the pace until you are sprinting away with the ball.

If the opponent runs alongside you, slow down and then suddenly pick up the pace again to leave them stranded. You can also wrong-foot opponents by pretending to stop the ball with the sole of your foot and dragging it in the same direction, accelerating away.

Swerving

This is a simple way to wrong-foot a defender. Drop a shoulder and look as if you intend to go off in one direction, for example to the right. As your opponent moves to the right to cover, swerve your body and pass on the left. If you carry this out correctly, the defender gets caught off-balance and cannot recover in time to challenge.

Feinting

One of the simplest ways (but often the most impressive to watch) of catching an opponent off-balance is by pretending to play the ball in one direction, but then playing it the opposite way. As an opponent moves to challenge, make a kicking motion. At the last second check the foot's kick and drag or push the ball in another direction.

In a match situation a player may feint to kick the ball hard, but instead suddenly swivels on the standing foot and turns the ball with the inside of the playing foot behind the standing leg.

Another good dummy, or feint, is to run with the ball and pretend to push it along with the outside of the foot, but instead pass the foot over the ball and drag it forwards with the inside of the other foot. Slow down, then accelerate as you play the ball with the inside of your foot.

TOP TIPS

DON'T GET MUGGED
Do not dribble the ball in your own penalty area. You could easily lose possession.

Speed is important, but so is close control. Regulate your pace to ensure you keep possession of the ball.

Do not use the same foot when dribbling. Juggle the ball from foot to foot, also varying your speed to keep opponents guessing.

Try not to get pushed out wide, or take on one opponent too many. Always look for the opportunity to catch out opponents by passing to a teammate.

Call a teammate by name as if you are going to pass. This diverts your opponent's attention long enough for you to take the ball past.

Look up and be aware of the players around you.

Evading a tackle

Be extremely careful when on the ball because defenders attempting to tackle you can, even accidentally, give you a very nasty injury if they kick you. As they lunge for the ball make sure neither you nor the ball is in the way.

SOCCER PRACTICE

- Set up a row of cones, garden sticks, or plastic bottles about six yards (5.5m) apart. Weave in and out of the cones with a ball, using the inside and outside of the foot. When you have reached the end of the obstacles, stop the ball with the sole of your boot, turn and go in the other direction. Time yourself and try to beat your best time.

  You can use this exercise on your own, or with a friend. If there are two of you, pass the ball to your partner once you have reached the end of the course. The partner plays the ball back to you so that you have to control it before setting off down the course again.

- Five players acting as forwards stand in a position about 12–15 yards (10–13m) outside the penalty area. Each is confronted by a defender standing just inside the area. Each attacker then runs at their respective opponents trying to dribble past into the area and shoot for goal. After time, defenders change places with offensive players.

Passing the ball

Once you can control the ball you need to learn about distribution—the art of keeping possession by linking with teammates through good, accurate passes. Passes can be made with the head or feet, on the ground or in the air, over long and short distances. You can even use your hands. A throw-in is a pass, and so is a throw-out by a goalkeeper.

Accurate passing of the ball is a skill. Spain's Xavi, when at his best, is a great distributor of the ball, especially in tight situations. Other examples of excellent passing players are Holland's Wesley Sneijder and Steven Gerrard of England.

When you're about to pass the ball you must carefully consider a number of possibilities before releasing it. If the ball is struck too hard it is difficult for the receiver to control it. If the ball is not struck sufficiently hard it could fail to reach its target and be intercepted by an opponent. If the ball is kicked into space for a teammate to run on to, your team could lose possession.

It is also important to look up when you are about to release the ball to see exactly where your teammates and opponents are. Like Xavi, Sneijder and Gerrard, good passers need control of the ball, accuracy, good balance and an awareness of the situation to ensure they don't give the ball away.

Basic technique

To pass accurately you have to be able to kick the ball well and with confidence, using the inside, outside or instep of your foot (or feet!). When passing, keep your eyes on the ball at the moment of impact, and use your arms for balance. Strike the ball in its middle for low passes. Strike it just below the center line for long, lofted passes. Follow through with the kicking foot in a deliberate, smooth action and with the non-kicking foot pointed in the direction you want the ball to go.

The side-foot or push pass

This is the most common and accurate way of passing to a teammate over a short distance. Your non-kicking foot should be on the ground alongside the ball. Look at the teammate you are about to pass to, then strike the ball in the center with the inside of your foot, keeping your body over the ball. Swing through with a pendulum movement from the hip to complete the pass.

SOCCER PRACTICE

- Playing in twos is an excellent way to practice basic passing, and to perfect that all-important accuracy at speed. Here are some handy training tips:

- Stand parallel to a teammate about four to five yards (4–5m) apart. Run up and down the field keeping your distance and passing the ball to each other. Each pass is made slightly ahead of the receiver so they can take the ball and play it in their stride. The receiver controls the ball using the inside of the far foot and passes it back in the next stride with the same foot. Repeat the exercise over a ten-minute spell, gradually increasing the distance between you and your partner.

- A good training exercise for four or more players involves interpassing in a triangular formation. Three players (A, B and C) pass to each other in a triangle. The ball is passed between any one of them and (D), who is continuing on the move and returns the ball to any one of the three players. They should remain alert in anticipation of (D) making a pass. Switch positions around after a few minutes.

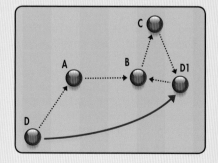

The long pass

As with the push pass, your non-kicking foot must be alongside the ball and pointing towards the player about to receive it. Use the instep to make the ball rise into the air. Keeping your ankle firm, lift back the kicking foot with toes pointed towards the ground and aim to strike the ball below the center line. As you strike the ball lean back and follow through to ensure it is hit with power.

The wall pass

Under pressure, or if you're closely marked, the wall pass—also known as a return pass—is useful. With the inside of your foot pass to a teammate who has moved away at an angle to you. As the teammate collects the ball, move away on the marker's blind side to accept a quick return pass in your stride, leaving your opponent stranded. In a sense, you have used your teammate as a wall to bounce the ball off. This is also known as the "one-two."

Running off the ball

There is no use passing the ball unless you have a teammate to pass it to. Successful moves and build-ups rely on unmarked players being in positions to receive the ball when they have run into space. They should then have time to control the ball and pass it on before being challenged. All good players have the vision to move into space to avoid being marked. Timing the run is vital—move too soon and you could find yourself offside or under heavy pressure when the pass is made to you.

INSET shows the side-foot, or push pass, where the ball is struck in the center with the inside of the foot, directing it accurately towards a teammate.

Power and accuracy are vital to the long pass. Note how the player's non-kicking foot is placed alongside the ball to help the shot's aim. The ball is kicked just below its center to loft it; the follow-through provides the power.

TOP TIPS

PASS AND RUN
After delivering a pass to a teammate, run into space to support and be ready to take a return pass. Many teams base their game on this simple tactic.

MAKE IT TOUGH FOR DEFENDERS
Try to keep yourself between the defender and the ball when passing to make a challenge difficult to deliver.

ON THE MOVE
Always run into space when you haven't got the ball. You will be much more difficult to mark and you'll be in a position to receive a pass without being challenged.

FOOT TALK
Remember the instep is used to achieve power, the inside of the foot for accuracy and the outside of the foot to swerve the ball and catch your opponent off-guard. The stronger and straighter the follow-through, the greater the power and accuracy.

Tackling

Fluid passing, scorching shooting and nifty ball-control all look great, but to achieve them you have to have the ball! This is where the less glamorous but vital art of tackling is paramount.

Often to win the ball you must tackle an opponent. A good tackle is a hard but fair challenge on the player with the ball. Like passing, shooting and dribbling, tackling requires skill and technique. Expert tacklers not only win the ball, but can set up a counter-attack immediately after. USA star Oguchi Onyewu is a top defender. He's very strong in the tackle but is also a superb reader of the game. Once he's won the ball his distribution is top class. Argentina's Javier Mascherano is also a brilliant winner and distributor of the ball.

But tackling does not only concern defenders or ball-winning midfielders. Every player on the field, including the goalkeeper, should learn and practice the art of winning the ball cleanly. There are three basic methods of tackling an opponent: the front block; the side block; and the sliding tackle.

Basic technique

Don't look at your opponent. Keep your eyes on the ball and use the side of your foot to make contact with it. Challenge for the ball when you are confident of winning it. Timing is vital to avoid missing the ball and striking your opponent. Clumsy challenges will be penalized by the referee, so be accurate. Put the whole of your leg and weight into the tackle and go in with determination. Hesitation, or relaxing your body, could result in your opponent brushing you aside or you could suffer a serious injury.

It's worth remembering that certain methods of tackling are determined by a defender's position or the attacking line of approach by an opponent.

The front block tackle

This is the strongest form of tackling. It is used when two players going for the ball reach it at the same time. It's also known in the game as going for a 50/50 ball. As your opponent tries to play the ball, close in and use the side of your foot to

In a 50/50 ball situation, the front block tackle is the most powerful means of gaining possession. The inside of the foot is used to block the ball, and then scoop it away from the challenger. In all tackling situations look at the ball, not at your opponent.

Use the side block tackle to take the ball off an opponent running in the same direction as yourself.

block the ball firmly. When you've made contact with the ball, ensure your body weight is on the tackling leg. Leaning a shoulder towards your opponent adds strength to your challenge.

The side block tackle

The side block tackle is used to take the ball off an opponent running in the same direction as yourself. When tackling an opponent from an angle, or the side, you must put all your weight on the tackling leg and slightly bend your supporting leg. As you make contact with the ball, turn and lean forward in the direction of the tackle.

The sliding tackle

The aim of the sliding tackle is not so much to gain possession of the ball, but to deflect it away from your opponent to a teammate, or safely out of play. This is a difficult tackling skill to perfect. To win the ball

It is important to keep your eye on the ball when challenging an opponent.

SOCCER PRACTICE

- Use a small field with four offensive players against three defenders marking one-on-one. Throughout the game the spare attacker is only allowed to receive the ball from a back pass.

- Mark out a small area 10 yards (9m) square, or use the penalty area. Use three players. One tries to win the ball, while the other two pass it between them. Take it in turns to be the attacker.

- Stand as a pair facing each other one stride from the ball. Both of you place the left foot slightly behind and to the side of the ball. Then, using the right foot, make a block tackle at the ball. Increase the power of the tackle and switch to the other foot after a ten-minute spell.

- One player runs down the pitch in a straight line with the ball. After five yards (4.5m) another player runs in pursuit and attempts to gain possession of the ball with a fair slide tackle from behind, hooking the ball away with the attacking foot.

- Play three-a-side games in which the players must beat an opponent before passing the ball. This encourages dribbling and tackling.

- Set up two cones six yards (5.5m) apart. Player (A) stands between the cones while two others, (B and C), position themselves on either side ten yards (9m) away. Players (B) and (C) pass the ball to each other between the cones, while player (A) tries to intercept. This is a good defensive training exercise.

cleanly and not foul your opponent after committing yourself requires split-second timing.

Try to challenge for the ball with your stronger leg, aiming your foot slightly in front of it. Keeping your eyes firmly on the ball, bend your supporting leg and slide on the knee and shin of this leg, putting your weight behind the tackling foot—a straight arm helps support the body when the tackling foot stretches to play the ball. After deflecting, or blocking the ball, withdraw your foot to avoid tripping your opponent. Watch USA defender Christie Rampone in action. No one times the sliding tackle better, and she usually comes away with the ball.

The back-heel tackle

Get close to the player you intend tackling so that you are running side by side. With your eyes on the ball, raise the foot of the tackling leg and block the ball with your heel. Do not swing the leg backwards, but check as it makes contact with the ball, transferring your weight to the tackling foot.

The shoulder charge

Maneuver yourself into position by running alongside the player you are about to challenge. In a slightly crouching position, come shoulder to shoulder with your opponent, ensuring only your upper arm and shoulder makes contact and that the challenge is from the side, not behind.

When you make contact put all your weight into the shoulder and lean in with the supporting leg for balance. When your opponent is off-balance, use the side of the foot to attack and win the ball.

INSET: The back-heel tackle is like a back-heel kick, but the aim is to block the ball. However, it is a dangerous tackle to try.

In the shoulder charge the challenge must be from the side, using only the upper arm and shoulder to make contact. The object is to unbalance your opponent so that you can use the side of the foot to capture the ball.

BELOW: Although the defender is going to get the ball in the tackle, the offensive player will probably be brought down as they won't be able to lift their leg over the tackler. This should not be a foul, but it is a risky challenge.

Jockeying for position is a way of frustrating an opponent in possession of the ball, forcing a mistake so that you can go in for a tackle.

TOP TIPS

PERFECT TIMING
Timing is essential. Go in hard, but take the ball cleanly. A mistimed tackle can result in a foul and a free kick or penalty kick being awarded against you as well as getting a yellow or red card.

CONFIDENCE AND DETERMINATION
Always believe you are going to win the ball. Go in half-heartedly and you'll be pushed aside, or risk injury.

TACKLE IN TRAINING
Don't hold off tackling during training or five-a-side games. Some teams do this to avoid injuries. But you train as you play. If you stop tackling in training defenders can develop a bad habit of holding off or hesitating during a game, while forwards can get a false sense of security when in possession.

STAND UP
Don't dive in when tackling. Stay on your feet. You can't tackle effectively on the ground.

SIDE ON
The frontal stance—presenting most of your body to an opponent you're about to take on—is the best tackling method for young players. But when you gain experience, try experimenting with a diagonal stance. This forces moves in other directions and so makes opponents less confident on the ball.

Jockeying for position

You can stop an opponent in possession by jockeying, or closing them down, and setting up a tackle. Approach your opponent when they have the ball under control, but keep your eyes on the ball. As the opponent moves towards you, back off slowly, leaving as little space as possible to play the ball, or increase the pace of play. Keep your eyes on the ball and wait for a mistake or a turn. Some players are uncomfortable if they keep the ball too long. They get frustrated and take risks. When you feel confident of getting the ball, go firmly into the tackle. It is important to remain patient and to stay on your feet.

Heading the ball

Heading the ball is a vital facet of the game. It's also one of the most difficult skills to perfect. The most common fault among young players learning to head a soccer ball is fear—they are afraid of not connecting with the ball properly and getting hurt as a result.

Because it is not a natural action, it's unsurprising that you may reflexively close your eyes when heading the ball. The result is that you head the ball with the top of your head and not the forehead. Because the reflex action to close your eyes when an object approaches is natural, you shouldn't be ashamed of it. But conquering it is essential if you want to be a better player.

As with all techniques covered in this book, it is important to practice this skill until you are comfortable heading the ball. Although the techniques used to head the ball under different circumstances are similar, there are four distinct types of header: offensive; defensive; glancing; and cushion (or head trap).

Basic technique

Whatever type of header you perform, they all require confidence and perfect timing. Apart from the glancing header, the ball should be met with the forehead. This is the strongest part of the skull and is much harder and tougher than a soccer ball. By using your forehead, the eyes can follow the ball right to the moment of impact.

That's the theory behind heading, but what's it like in practice? It's important to keep your eyes on the ball as it drops towards you and to concentrate on directing the ball to the intended target. As the ball approaches, tense your neck muscles and move your head slightly back. To help you achieve a good contact, try imagining that you have a target painted on your forehead. When the ball comes into range, aim to meet it where the bullseye would be.

When you make contact with the ball, thrust your forehead forwards sharply. Follow through with your body, bending your elbows back to help add more power to the header.

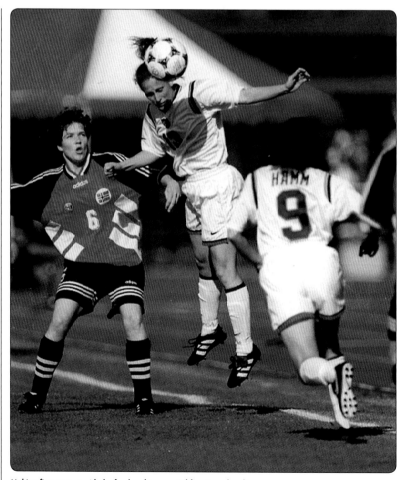

Making firm contact with the forehead is essential for strong heading.

SOCCER PRACTICE

- In threes: the players stand in a triangular formation about five yards (4.5m) apart. (A) throws the ball to (B), who heads the ball on to (C). (C) fields the ball, throws it to (A) who heads it to (B), and so on . . .
  In pairs: stand 12 yards (11m) apart. Throw the ball so that your partner can make a standing jump to head it back. Alternatively, stand 15 yards (13.7m) apart. Throw the ball so that your partner can run forward and jump to head it back.

- **Heading volley ball**
  Two six-a-side teams compete in heading the ball over a net seven feet (2m) high without letting the ball touch the ground. The ball is served by a player from the base-line of the court, striking it by hand to send it over the net. The ball is then headed back and forth over the net. If it drops to the ground, fails to go over the net, or goes out of play, the service or the point is lost to the other side. This game is particularly suited to indoor arenas.

ball, be ready to take advantage should the goalkeeper be poorly positioned. If the goalkeeper is off-balance when leaping to catch the ball, the offensive player has an advantage.

USA midfielder Landon Donovan has often proved himself a matchwinner for his country by timing his runs to arrive late in the penalty area and score with an attacking header. England's Wayne Rooney is also a great exponent of the attacking header.

Heading for goal
This may seem obvious, but it is worth remembering that if you head the ball downwards you have a high-percentage chance of hitting the target rather than ballooning the

This action gives the ball its impetus and, if your technique is good, should prevent you from getting hurt.

Cushion headers require less power than standard headers but the technique up until the moment of contact is the same. If you have to jump for the ball it is better to run forwards to meet it than wait for it to hit you. Leap into the air with your leading leg while running, since this gives you greater height than a standing two-footed jump. A word of caution; remember to keep your arms down when jumping. You don't need to use your elbows for leverage, and jumping at an opponent is a foul.

Offensive headers
The aim of the offensive header is to create havoc in the opposing penalty area and, hopefully, score. This header, like a shot at goal, should be aimed low, because it is the toughest attack for goalkeepers to save. When heading a crossed

HEADING: keep your eyes on the ball, sway back, then bring the head forwards and follow through with a strong punch.

German striker Miroslav Klose keeps his eyes on the ball as he glances it clear in this contested header.

Diving headers

Diving headers, when offensive players dive full length to head a low cross, often result in spectacular goals. They are also very hard to defend against. A diving header can also help a defender protect the goal, or clear their lines.

The technique used to perform the diving header is essentially the same as that used for other headers, but there are three important points to stress:

(1) throw your arms out in front, below the height of your shoulders, to add power to your dive;

2) make contact with your forehead and not the top of the head;

3) bend your knees and relax your arms to help cushion your fall.

Defensive headers

Defenders must be able to head the ball powerfully and accurately when the team is under pressure. And they must be strong enough to reach it before an opponent, especially in a crowded penalty area.

Don't wait for the ball to drop when heading in defense—attack it as it arrives, jumping and striking the ball with the middle of your forehead. Don't worry about opponents. Pay too much attention to them instead of the ball, and you'll lose concentration.

Jumping for the ball

Lean forwards to gain height as you jump. Before heading the ball, arch your back and flex your neck and shoulder muscles. When you're in the air try to hit the ball at the highest point of your jump. Make contact with the center of the ball and hammer your head and neck forward in one movement to add power to the header.

ball over the crossbar. This is the main reason why defenders head the ball up while attackers head down.

The vast majority of headers on goal come from either crosses or other glanced headers (which are discussed later). In a crowded penalty area positioning is vital. When launching yourself at the ball be aware of the location of your opponents, the goalkeeper and, most importantly, the goal.

If you're outside the penalty area, judge the flight of the ball, run, jump and head it towards the point you calculate will take it in front of goal.

When heading from a cross, steer the ball back in the direction from which it came, aiming for the near post. If you use this method there's a good chance the goalkeeper may be unsighted and out of position. And don't forget the golden rule: headers aimed downwards are much more accurate than balls headed in the air.

With the diving header, make sure that your arms are well forward and the knees bent for a softer fall.

To get the required power and height into a jump, good timing is essential. Even a short run-up and a single-foot take-off will give you greater height than you can achieve by making a standing jump with both feet.

In defense, if you're covering an opponent from behind and you need to jump vertically for a high ball, you should stand slightly away from the player you are marking. This gives you space to run forwards when making a jump for the ball. It also prevents you from making bodily contact with your opponent and committing a foul.

The glancing header

The forehead is used to deflect the ball in different directions when performing a glancing header (or flick-on). Remember, you can use the force of the ball to redirect it away from an opponent, or towards the goal. The forehead acts as a block, or glancing surface, off which to bounce the ball.

When you've made contact with the ball, twist your head and body in the direction you want it to go. The harder you strike the ball with your forehead, the more power and pace your glancing header will have. This can prove decisive in front of goal.

TOP TIPS

EYE ON THE BALL
Remember, once you have decided to go for a header don't change your mind! Attack the ball by getting in front of your opponent. Watch the ball right up to the moment of impact.

DON'T DUCK
Do not head the ball if it is below your waist (except for diving headers)—you might get kicked in the face by an opponent.

TIME YOUR JUMPS
Good heading usually involves jumping. A well-timed leap helps you with high balls and gives you a big advantage over your opponents.

BACKWARDS DANGER
Avoid heading the ball when running backwards. You will not be able to jump for the ball, or generate enough power or control over your header.

With the glancing header, also referred to as "deflecting the ball," use your head and body to glance the ball in the desired direction.

Throw-ins

Essentially, a throw-in is a method of restarting play. But in the modern game it is also used as a tactical weapon to create scoring chances, and in this respect it is an important skill to perfect.

Taking a throw-in ought to be easy, especially as there are 20–40 awarded during every match. Despite this frequency, it's amazing how many players commit foul throws, giving the advantage to the opposition.

Before playing, assign players in your team to take the throw-ins. Confusion over who is going to take a throw-in can lose vital seconds, while the opposition can regroup. The last thing a coach wants to see is teammates arguing among themselves over who is to take a throw-in—and conversely you don't need the team confused because no one steps forward to take the throw.

If you are going to call for the ball from a throw-in you should always move around. The more space you can create, the more difficult you are to mark and close down. And when you are throwing in select a teammate to throw at, or throw the ball into space for your selected teammate to run on to.

It's useful to remember that if you receive a ball from a throw-in when you're in an attacking position you cannot be offside.

Basic technique

Stand with both feet on or behind the touchline at the point where the ball went out of play when taking a throw-in. Both hands must be on the ball as you throw from behind and over your head. You may raise your heels but a part of each foot must remain firmly on the ground. When throwing the ball, it is advisable to stand just behind the touchline. This helps you avoid putting one, or both feet on to the Field of Play.

The long throw

This can be a useful offensive option anywhere within 30 yards (27.5m) of your opponent's penalty area and can be as effective as a corner kick. The long throw is used prominently in the British game. In the rest of the world and at international level, teams usually rely on the short, quick throw.

Republic of Ireland defender Rory Delap has become an expert of the long throw into the opponent's

SOCCER PRACTICE

- **In pairs:** one player sits down, the other stands up five yards (4.5m) away. The standing player throws the ball to the sitting player who catches it and throws it back from behind the head.

- **In pairs:** stand with feet astride, ten yards (9m) apart. Throw a ball overhead to each other. After a few minutes do the same but with one foot forwards. This enables you to put more pace on the ball.

- **In pairs:** your partner throws a ball to you. Control it with your head, chest or feet before kicking it back. If the ball bounces before reaching the partner, switch roles.

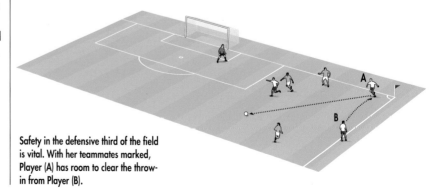

Safety in the defensive third of the field is vital. With her teammates marked, Player (A) has room to clear the throw-in from Player (B).

In the long throw-in, the hands should be placed behind the ball to provide more power. Lean well back with one leg extended behind the throw, but still ensuring both feet remain on the ground and on or behind the touchline.

TOP TIPS

DON'T LET THE BALL BOUNCE

Throw the ball to the receiver's head, chest or feet—don't throw it in front of them, unless it is downfield for them to run on to. If the ball bounces it will be more difficult to control.

DUMMY RUNS

If you are about to receive the ball from a throw-in, move as if you are going to run in one direction, but then quickly switch and move in another. Your marker will be caught off-guard and you'll create extra space to receive the ball from the thrower.

CONCENTRATE

Always concentrate on the basics. Lifting a foot, or failing to take the ball behind the head results in a foul throw—why make it easy for the opposition to gain possession?

QUICK RETURN

You can retain possession if the receiver plays the ball straight back to the player who has just taken the throw-in.

KICK-INS

One experiment being carried out in some parts of the world is the kick-in. As its name suggests, players kick the ball back into play instead of throwing it. In the 1994–95 season, kick-ins were used in the Diadora League in England, while in Belgium and Hungary second division teams tried out this new concept.

danger areas and it has proved to be a decisive offensive weapon.

For long throws, the hands should be placed behind the ball (not on the side as for a normal throw-in) to give it extra power, height and distance. Lean back as far as you can, remembering to keep both feet on the ground behind the touchline, and lift your heels off the ground. Tense your stomach muscles and heave your body forwards, swinging the arms powerfully over your head. With a final flick of the fingers, propel the ball high into the danger-zone.

The long throw-in can also be used by defenders to throw the ball back to the goalkeeper, or down the touchline for an offensive teammate to run on to.

Strong stomach muscles and powerful shoulders are essential to achieve an effective long throw-in.

The short, quick throw-in

A short throw-in taken quickly can be just as effective as a long throw. It is used to get the ball back into play, to keep possession, set up offensive opportunities and catch opponents off-guard.

Goalkeeping

Goalkeeping is a highly specialized role, demanding specialist skills. This is the most important member of the team, playing in the most demanding and difficult position of all. They are under constant pressure to play well because the slightest mistake can be cruelly punished and result in a goal being scored, or even worse, defeat. Outfield players can afford to have an off day, make the occasional mistake, misplaced pass, or shoot wide of the target. But not goalkeepers.

Good goalkeeping is an art and many leading professional clubs employ ex-keepers as coaches to pass on their knowledge and experience.

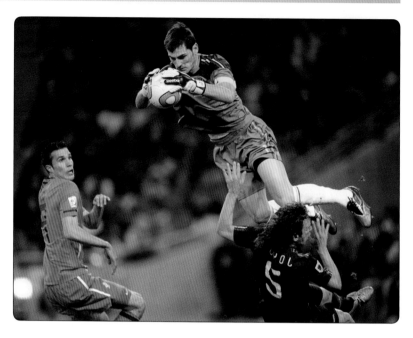

Goalkeepers must be strong, agile, brave and commanding—one mistake could cost your team the match.

A goalkeeper should be tall, with strong hands and shoulders. They need to possess the agility of a gymnast, the reflexes of a tennis star, the strength and courage of a football player and the ball-handling skills of a basketball player. The best keepers are also commanding and aggressive on the field with an unflappable temperament. It requires someone who can keep their emotions under control if they have made a mistake and not allow it to affect their teammates. A temperamental keeper can be a liability because anger and frustration will unsettle the defenders in front of their.

But an extrovert keeper's antics can be positive. Paraguay's former World Cup goalkeeper Jose-Luis Chilavert was the captain of his national side and scored many a goal from free kicks and penalties. Tim Howard, the USA's national goalkeeper, is unflappable in his own box, but he is also known for joining his team's offense at a corner if they are losing late in an important game.

The most extroverted goalkeeper of all time must be Colombia's Rene Higuita. He often came out of his goal to dribble the ball down the wing, or tackle an opponent outside his penalty area. He often operated as a spare sweeper. But he lived too dangerously during the 1990 World Cup finals against Cameroon when he lost the ball to Roger Milla, who went on to score.

In the modern game, as a goalkeeper you are required to do more than just stop shots. The position provides an excellent view of the game and you must have the vision to create moves by distributing the ball, by feet or hand, to teammates in good strategic positions.

LEFT: face straight on to the ball when catching a high shot.

CENTER: cradle the ball and cushion its impact when dealing with chest- or waist-height threats.

RIGHT: in the low catch, use a raised knee to block the ball's path as you catch it.

Catching the ball at waist height

When stopping shots at waist height, the whole body should be behind the line of the ball, with the palms of the hands pointed upwards so the ball can be scooped and gathered safely into the chest, which should be relaxed on impact to cushion the power of the shot. Wrap your hands around the ball and bend your chest forwards over it. This helps prevent the ball slipping out of your grasp.

Catching the ball at chest height

To prevent the ball bouncing off your chest when catching it, place both hands behind it when making contact. The elbows should be kept close to the body and the fingers outspread.

Catching the ball above the head

Dealing with high balls and crosses is probably the most important aspect of your goalkeeper's role after stopping shots. You have a distinct advantage over your opponents because you can use your hands, and will be already on the move as the ball comes across enabling you to jump much higher.

You should try to take the ball at its highest point and not wait for it to drop. Get into position using short steps and carefully watching the flight of the ball, take off with a spring, getting your arms up early and high, with both hands behind the ball and fingers outspread. After catching the ball firmly with hands wrapped around it, clutch it to your chest, protecting it as you hit the ground. This helps you hold on to the ball if an opponent makes a challenge, or crashes into you.

Basic techniques

The basic principle of goalkeeping is safety first. This means getting both hands on the ball, with the body behind the hands to form a second barrier. Keeping balanced is most important, but your position varies with the height, speed and direction of the ball as it comes to you. This goes not only for your body and legs, but also for your arms and hands.

Stopping a ground shot

There are two ways of stopping a shot fired along the ground: the stooping catch and the kneeling gather. For the stoop, make sure you are in direct line with the flight of the ball. Keep your legs straight and bend down at the waist. Place the hands and palms upwards with the little fingers together under the ball and scoop the ball firmly upwards into the chest, grasping it tightly with both hands.

To gather a shot in the kneeling position, move the lower half of the body and feet sideways into line with the ball. Lower one knee to the ground, level with the opposite heel, and turn your chest towards the ball to form a wider barrier. Keeping your head steady and eyes on the ball, scoop the ball into the chest as before.

TOP TIPS

BODY BEHIND THE BALL
Make sure you're fully behind the ball by moving your body and feet before getting your hands into position. Once your feet are in position, the body naturally follows.

CONCENTRATE!
Retain concentration for the whole game. You could go for 88 minutes without having a shot to save and then, in the 89th minute, have to deal with an attacker running at you, or a dangerous high cross. Think positively all the time and don't be distracted.

ATTITUDE
Never change your mind, or flap at the ball. Go for it positively, ignoring the other players around you.

Punching and deflecting the ball

There are times when a goalkeeper under pressure, in a crowded penalty area or goalmouth, is forced to punch the ball away, deflect it over the crossbar, or around a post.

Because of their vulnerability against tall attackers, smaller goalkeepers may prefer to punch the ball away when dealing with high crosses. A two-fisted punch is best used when the ball is coming straight at you. With clenched fists make contact with the center of the ball and send it back in the direction it came from.

When using one fist, use the arm nearest the goal line and don't swing at the ball. The punching action should again be as straight

as possible. Make sure you punch with the knuckles and aim to fist the ball as high in the air as possible. If you punch the ball out at head height, or below, the ball could drop to an opponent in a good scoring position.

On occasions during a game you may not be sure of getting two hands on the ball and may prefer to palm or deflect it over the crossbar. Leap as if to catch the ball, but with a natural overarm swing, spread the palm and fingers to make a good contact and guide it over the crossbar. Be ready to stretch your arm and fingertips and dive full length if the shot is particularly powerful, or at an angle. You should aim to reach the ball before it drops below the level of the crossbar, but if the shot is dipping below the bar two hands might be needed. Time your jump to give an upwards thrust to the hands, which should be close together and bent slightly backwards.

To deflect a ball around a post, follow the flight right on to the palm of your hand. Tense your wrist at the moment of impact to cushion the power of the ball and guide it around the upright.

Diving at a striker's feet

Timing is crucial to good handling, especially when diving at an offensive player's feet in a 1-v-1 situation to smother the ball with the body. Courage is part of a goalkeeper's job, and a great deal of it is needed when diving at the feet of an opponent who's broken through into the area. Injuries can occur if a keeper hesitates or uses the wrong technique.

As you come out to face your attacker, get into a low position with knees bent, head and shoulders forward and arms in front of your head. Get as low to the ground as possible when going for the ball so that your body is a yard (1m) or so behind it. Make sure your timing is right. If you dive too soon the offensive player can lift the ball over your body; dive too late and the ball could slip under your body.

Smothering the ball: the body curls protectively around the ball. Keep your head protected from a flying cleat.

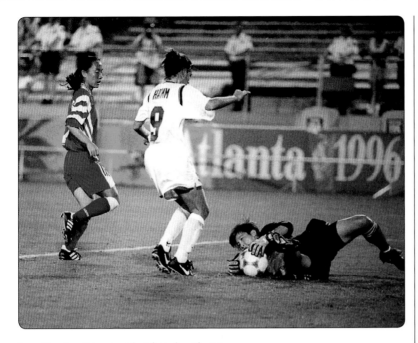

Be positive when diving at a striker's feet—do not hesitate.

Goal kicks

There are three types of goal kick:

(1) The simple big kick over the halfway line so that your offensive player can challenge for possession.

(2) The short kick to one of your defenders to bring other teammates into play and start a move.

(3) The chipped kick to loft the ball over opposing offensive players to a teammate in space.

Accuracy is more important than brute force with goal kicking. Keep your eyes on the ball and head down. To gain more height run up at an angle and get your cleat under the ball. If you want to get the ball as far downfield as possible run straight at it and kick through.

Also make sure your body is along the ground at an angle before reaching for the ball. Get your body as close to the ball as you can when grabbing it from the offensive player's feet and clutching it into your chest. Your head should be protected as it is tucked behind your hands, arms and legs, well away from the ball.

Kicking the ball from your hands

Like all good outfield players, goalkeepers should be able to use both feet and have the strength to kick the ball half the length of the field.

Only being able to kick with one foot can be a great tactical disadvantage, especially if opponents force you to use your weaker foot to kick out from the penalty area.

When kicking from the hand keep your eyes on the ball and throw it well up in front of you. Be careful not to throw it too close to your body because that restricts your movements, or too far away so you have to stretch for it. Keep your head down and follow through with the kicking leg. Your body should be behind the line of the ball to avoid being off-balance and slicing your kick.

Throwing the ball out

When you've saved the ball, look up and see if a teammate is in a good position to start a move. If so, you might decide to throw the ball out rather than kick it. Throwing is the most accurate way of distributing the ball and keeping possession with your team. Roll the

The overarm throw and the underhand roll.

SOCCER PRACTICE

- **Using four or five players:** stand in your goal facing the strikers who are positioned around the edge of the penalty area. The strikers take it in turns to shoot at goal. After saving the shot, get back on to your feet as quickly as possible. To improve your speed, the next striker shoots at goal immediately after the previous shot is saved. Vary the exercise by trying chip shots.

- **In pairs:** place a cone to act as a defender at an angle to the goal just inside the penalty area. Your partner runs up and dummies past the cone and shoots for goal. You come out to narrow the angle and attempt to save the shot. The attacker should vary direction around the cone and shoot with the other foot. Gradually move the cone closer to the goal.

- **In pairs:** stand on the goal line with your back to your partner taking the kick. The kicker shouts "ready" as contact with the ball is made. Twist to face the shot and save it. Now throw the ball back to the kicker. Repeat the exercise using different types of shot to keep you alert.

- **In pairs:** sit on the ground three or four yards (3m) away from a partner who throws the ball towards you at varying heights and speed. As soon as it leaves your partner's hands, leap and try to save the ball.

- **In pairs:** stand in the middle of a goal, or between two cones placed seven or eight yards (7m) apart. Your partner, 12 yards (11m) away, rolls the ball five yards (4.5m) to your left or right. You dive to try to save the ball. After a while, get your partner to roll the ball directly towards you. Race out from your line and dive forwards to smother the ball.

- **In threes:** to practice taking high balls, turning them over the bar or punching them away. The ball is thrown, or crossed into the goalmouth by one player, while another challenges the goalkeeper's attempts to catch the ball.

ball out underarm if your teammate is standing fairly close to you. You need to roll the ball into space just in front of the player so that it can be controlled.

The overarm throw is used to distribute the ball over a greater distance. Use your non-throwing arm to point at the player you are throwing the ball to. This helps your balance. Keep your feet apart, head and body in line with the target and throwing arm straight. Bowl the ball overarm with plenty of power.

Time

Remember the goalkeeper cannot take more than six seconds while holding, bouncing, or throwing the ball. Once the ball has been released, it cannot be touched with the keeper's hands until another player has been in contact with it. If this "six seconds law" is broken, an indirect free kick is awarded and with it the threat of a strike at goal from within the penalty area.

The back-pass rule has been dealt with on pages 16–17.

Dealing with penalty kicks

At a penalty kick the odds are heavily stacked in favor of the penalty taker. The goalkeeper is not expected to make a save. They are heroes if that happens.

Despite the odds, knowing how to deal with spotkicks is becoming more important now that we have penalty shootouts deciding the results of many games.

Remember, the pressure is all on the penalty taker, so try to gain a psychological advantage by looking confident as the player shapes up to take the kick. Attempt to close your mind to all the noise around you and concentrate on the ball. As the penalty taker places the ball try to assess which side of the goal it's going to go.

If a right-footed player uses a straight run-up they are more likely to place the ball to your left. If a left-footed player uses a straight run-up they are likely to place the ball to your right. If the kicker runs at an angle, chances are they are going to bend the ball with pace in the same direction they are running. A blaster will try to hit the ball high into the net.

But whatever method the kicker is using stay on your line and in an upright position for as long as you can. Move your body a little so you are in a position to shift your feet quickly when you have decided in which direction you are going to

Goalkeeping can be tough, especially when opposing players collide with you. But a controlled keeping technique can minimize injury.

throw yourself. But don't be too disappointed if you fail to make a save.

Learning the angles

Good positioning is a vital part of a goalkeeper's game and one of the most difficult skills to learn. Shots are easier to save with good positioning. Goals are easily scored if a goalkeeper stands rooted to a spot on the goal line. The aim is for the goalkeeper to appear as a large obstacle to an opponent and ensure that as little of the goal can be seen by the attacker as possible.

To do this the goalkeeper must come off the line and move towards the attacker, narrowing the angle of the target area. Timing is important. Come out too far or too soon and attackers dribble the ball around you; come out too slowly or not far enough and the attacker can come in

close with a large target to aim for.

It's also important to remain on your feet with arms outstretched, presenting as large a barrier as possible to block the attacker's route to goal.

If the attacker runs in from the flank, move across to narrow the angle and position yourself on the near side of the goal so you have the space to stop a cross.

Top goalkeepers are brilliant at getting themselves in the correct position for any situation. They often make great saves look easy because they have positioned themselves in exactly the right spot to take the ball cleanly. Spectacular goalkeepers are rarely the best goalkeepers.

During corner kicks you should position yourself towards the post further away from the ball. You will then have space to be able to move forwards when the ball is kicked.

TOP TIPS

PUNCHING CLEAR
Young goalkeepers should always punch the ball in the direction they are facing. Experienced keepers with strong hands and arms can use the back of the hand to knock the ball to safety.

WARM-UP
Before a game it's important for goalkeepers to warm-up with gentle stretching exercises. Then get teammates to launch balls at you from all angles, heights and distances.

WEIGHTS
Weight training, under supervision, helps strengthen your arms, shoulders, wrists and thighs—all essential parts of the body for a keeper.

COMMUNICATION
As goalkeeper you are in command of the penalty area. Make sure your defenders are aware of attackers moving into space, or making blind-side runs, and shout loudly when you are going for crosses. This way you can avoid any confusion.

ATTACK! ATTACK!
Keepers don't just defend. You can set up an offense by distributing the ball quickly, either by kicking, or throwing it out. A long kick upfield can catch out opposing defenses, and a quick throw to a winger or midfielder can start an offensive move before the opposition has a chance to reorganize.

TACTICS

Young players should concentrate on learning the basic soccer skills, but as you progress it is essential to have an understanding of the formations and patterns of play. Soccer is a team game and the manager, or coach, should decide on a system that makes the best use of the players available. A good playing system uses players' strengths and covers up their weaknesses.

But systems alone do not win games. It is the players working within the team formation who get the results. So, it's important that the manager, or coach, explains the system to all the players in the squad to ensure they are familiar and happy with their roles.

No system, nor tactics, should ignore the individual talents of the team's more skilled players. Everyone likes to see players performing their magic in games, but those skills should be used for the benefit of the whole team.

Basically, tactics are plans from which teams work to get the ball into the opposing danger area to score goals and to stop their opponents from doing the same.

Before the great Hungarians defeated England 6–3 at Wembley in 1953 with a new style of play, the then-prevalent English game was based on 2–3–5 formation: a goalkeeper, two fullbacks, a center-half, two half-backs and five forwards.

The Hungarians played with a center-forward deep in midfield and with two offensive inside-forwards. The England center-half was pulled out of position, while the two fullbacks stayed deep which gave the Hungarian inside-forwards Kocsis and Puskas space in which to cause havoc.

The result shocked world soccer and within a few years the Hungarian style of play had completely revolutionized the game. Instead of kick-and-rush, tactics and systems evolved which enabled teams to make better use of their players.

The Brazilian World Cup-winning team in 1958 used four defenders across the back to deny the opposing wingers space. From this start, teams began to play with four players in offense and two in midfield. So the 4–2–4 and then 4–3–3 systems were born.

Throughout the 1960s and 1970s the game became more defensive with fewer attackers and more players in midfield. Tactics were amended and devised accordingly.

These days World Cups have been won with teams using five players in midfield with just one attacker, as Argentina did in 1986.

Some clubs have used a sweeper with three defenders at the back, five in midfield and one man at the front as the lone striker. The reason for this defensive formation is simple: flooding the midfield makes it difficult for opponents to mark the midfielders.

Modern systems work successfully because players are more flexible, with midfield players and strikers often being required to move back to help out in defense, while defenders often support the offense with runs down the flanks.

Soccer is an easy game to play, but tactics and systems are becoming more and more sophisticated as managers or coaches continually work out plans to outwit their opponents.

So a study of team tactics and formations will help to improve your skills and provide a better understanding of the modern game and how it should be played at all levels.

Modern players must possess a knowledge of tactics as well as ability.

Team formations

A team positions its players in any one of the 17 positions shown in Diagram A. The choice of formation depends on the system chosen by the manager, or coach. All systems should be flexible to take into account weather conditions, the opposition, the competition, venue and players.

On hard, icy surfaces smaller players will keep their footing better than taller ones because of their lower center of gravity; in wet, muddy conditions strength is required; and players not fully fit could struggle on a hot afternoon.

There is no use playing 4–4–2, if the opposition is playing that way, unless you want to cancel each other out. Good coaches do their homework and use tactics to counter opponents. They work out the opposition's strengths and weaknesses before the game. If the opposing winger is their star player the coach will not want to have a young, inexperienced fullback marking him.

If a team is playing in a cup competition over

Diagram A

1. Goalkeeper
2. Sweeper
3. Right back
4. Right centerback
5. Left centerback
6. Left back
7. Right half/wing back
8. Central defender
9. Left half/wing back
10. Right midfield
11. Center midfield
12. Left midfield
13. Right winger
14. Right striker
15. Central striker
16. Left striker
17. Left winger

two legs, a draw might be good enough. So, the coach may play a defensive formation, especially if the game is away from home. Teams generally prefer to play offensive tactics at home, on familiar ground in front of their own supporters. If players are injured, the coach may decide to change the tactics slightly to suit the players available.

4-2-4
Different nations tend to play different techniques. For example, 30 years ago, most English clubs used a 4–2–4 or 4–3–3 system. The benefit of 4–2–4 (Diagram B) is that you can have six players attacking, or defending. When defending, two midfield players pull back to help the defense. When attacking they can move forwards to support the offense. You would also be looking for the two fullbacks to break forwards in support. The success of this formation depends on the ability and stamina of the midfielders to continually link with offense and defense. This is a good system to adopt if your team has fast wingers and the players are able to distribute long, accurate passes to the strikers.

4-3-3
This system (Diagram C) gives you strength through the midfield as you have three players in this area. You can also use seven defensive players and six in offense,

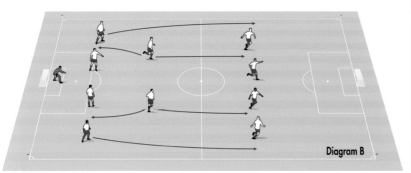

Diagram B

depending on which team has the ball. When your team is in possession the three midfield players can make late forward runs, adding more power to the offense. Use this system if your team likes to build offenses with passes.

4-4-2

This defensive formation (Diagram D), is often used when a team has a shortage of strikers, or a surplus of midfielders. It allows you to get eight players behind the ball when defending. When you are attacking there are four players available to support the strikers with the two wide midfield players being used as wingers. Great strain is put on the two strikers, who must be able to hold the ball under pressure until their midfielders can support them.

5-3-2

The sweeper system (Diagram E) is a defensive formation used for absorbing relentless pressure and launching quick counter-offenses. Although primarily defensive, used correctly it can become an effective offensive formation. When the opportunity arises, the two fullbacks push forward to support the three midfielders. Many top European teams such as Barcelona have used this system with slight variations.

4-5-1

An ultra-defensive system (Diagram F) which is very difficult for teams to break down. When attacking, the ball has to be passed accurately and the midfield players have to break forward to support the striker. At international level, France won the European Championship in 1984 under Michel Platini's captaincy, with five in midfield and a lone striker in offense.

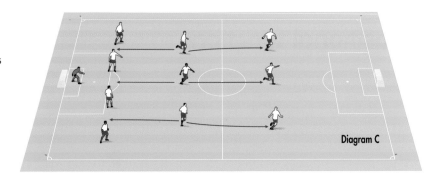

Diagram C

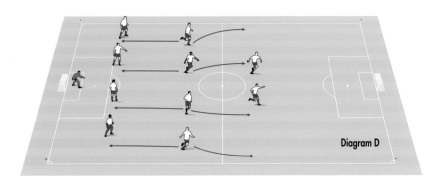

Diagram D

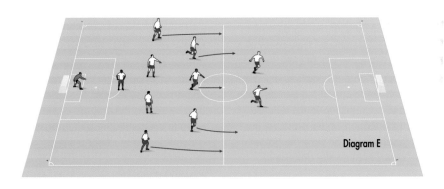

Diagram E

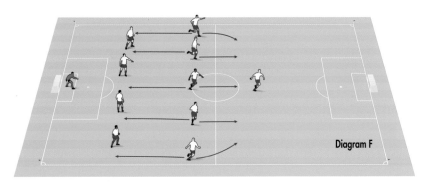

Diagram F

Positional functions

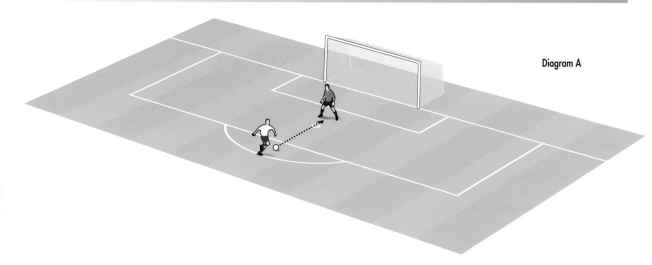

Diagram A

The prime function of the goalkeeper is to stop goals being scored against their team. However, they are more than the last line of defense, they can be the springboards for offense. The keeper should start an offensive movement by throwing the ball to a nearby teammate. They could also use a long kick upfield to catch the opposition out. Goalkeepers should take command of the penalty area and keep talking to the defense. If the team is under pressure, the goalkeeper can slow the game down to allow the defense to

regroup before releasing the ball. But don't get a yellow card for time-wasting.

Because of their position, goalkeepers have a panoramic view of the whole Field of Play and can spot problems building up for defenders. They can also see offensive opportunities when spaces occur, or when teammates are left unmarked. The keeper can also act as a sweeper, moving out of the penalty area with the ball to pass to a defender, or midfield player in space.

Remember, the keeper's positional skills are also vital at all corner kicks, dead-ball situations—especially when organizing a defensive wall—and when the opposition is attacking.

A goalkeeper must also be ready for the unexpected, such as a rebound, sliced kick, mistimed pass by a defender, or a snap shot from an opposing striker.

Diagram A shows where a goalkeeper should be positioned to narrow the angle and reduce the target area a striker has to aim at.

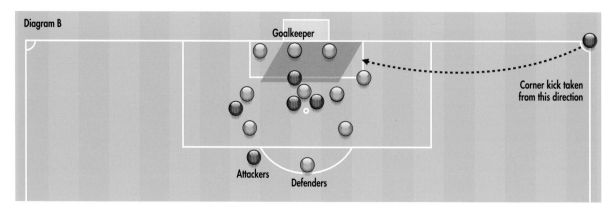

Diagram B

Goalkeeper

Corner kick taken from this direction

Attackers

Defenders

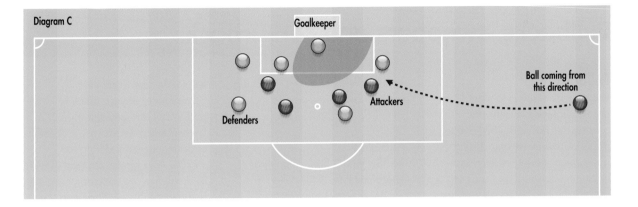

Diagram C

A goalkeeper is expected to gather all high balls in the goal area. Diagram B shows where the keeper should be positioned for a corner kick taken from the right. If you're playing as the keeper, you should be in the ideal position to cover the shaded area. Your defenders can adjust their positions to counter the danger when the ball is crossed.

For a fierce drive, or cross to the near post, you should be positioned a yard (1m) or so off the goal line (as in Diagram C) from where you can see the danger and follow the flight of the ball more easily. Notice how the defenders have moved to cover the shaded danger zone behind the keeper. You can even move a defender to stand on the goal line.

A goalkeeper is responsible for organizing the defense for free kicks around the penalty area. This must be done quickly. In Diagram D, a free kick has been awarded about 25 yards (23m) from goal. The goalkeeper has positioned a wall of four defenders ten yards (9m) from the ball, with Player (A) standing slightly outside a line between the ball and the near post. If the keeper's line of vision is reduced, it may be better to take Player (B) out of the wall. The goalkeeper now has a large area of goal covered and can move forward, or along the goal line to save the ball if it gets past the wall.

The goalkeeper is responsible for organizing the defense for free kicks directed into the penalty box.

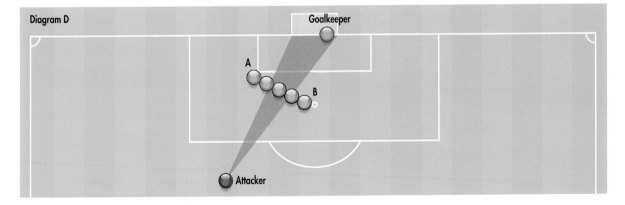

Diagram D

Fullbacks, sweepers and centerbacks

Fullback

The fullback's task is to mark, cover and tackle. Essentially, playing this position, you have to stop offensive moves by closing down the opposing winger and force the offense to go inside to prevent the ball being crossed into the goal area.

You should also cover your centerback, protect the goalkeeper, clear the keeper's lines when under pressure, support the midfield and link up with the wingers. Modern fullbacks also attack down the flanks and get crosses in at every opportunity.

Examples of two excellent attacking fullbacks are Ashley Cole of Engand and Brazil's Maicon.

You also need to have the pace to match the winger you're marking. If you have no wide player to cover, you should support your defensive partners and look out for opposing players making late runs so that you can block their path to goal.

Sweeper

The "Sweeper" (Diagram A), or "libero" as this role is called in Europe, does not have to mark anyone in particular. When playing this roving role behind the back three or four, you should be ready to intercept attackers who have made late runs past the central defenders. As a sweeper, you should be ready to collect or "sweep-up" any loose balls. You should also be a good tackler, header of the ball, passer and reader of the game. From the sweeper's position behind the back four you should be able to spot offensive moves building up. The sweeper can also perform a vital offensive role. Generally you are unmarked and know exactly where teammates are positioned.

The former Bayern Munich and West Germany star, Franz Beckenbauer, was a very successful attacking sweeper during the 1970s. As a former midfield player, Beckenbauer was able to collect the ball deep in his own half and then set off on a run, or start an attacking move with a long, accurately flighted pass.

Excellent distribution is a vital factor and both Gerard Pique of Spain and Germany's Philipp Lahm are outstanding examples.

Centerback

Most teams have two centerbacks who are the kingpins of defense. In this position you're covering the area where attackers most want to be and so you are under almost as much pressure as the goalkeeper. Any mistake you make could lead to a goal. You must develop a firm understanding with your centerback partner. It is important that each of you knows when the other is about to make a challenge, so either can provide support. The taller of the two normally takes the more central position because of the obvious advantage in the air dealing with crosses and defensive headers. The other centerback will play diagonally behind, ready to deal with movements along the ground.

Power in the air is essential for centerbacks. You must completely dominate the strikers

Sweepers and central defenders must be ever alert —cutting out danger at the first opportunity.

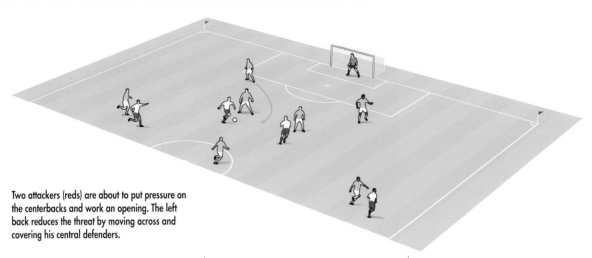

Two attackers (reds) are about to put pressure on the centerbacks and work an opening. The left back reduces the threat by moving across and covering his central defenders.

you're marking, especially in the penalty area. Often this means giving away a corner, instead of heading the ball out into space where an alert opponent can seize on the clearance and shoot for goal, or maintain the pressure by crossing back in the danger zone. Centerbacks must have the pace to move forwards in offense and to recover if they get caught out of

position, or mistime a tackle. If you are the taller player you will often support offenses at corner kicks, where your aerial power can do a great deal of damage. Players in this position often make ideal captains. Franco Baresi of Italy and Bobby Moore of England's 1966 World Cup-winning team were excellent examples of captains who led their team by example.

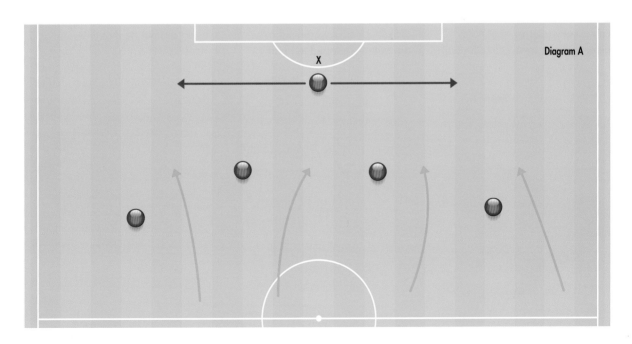

Diagram A

The sweeper (X) supports the back four. The blue arrows show potential runs by attacking players.

Midfielders

The midfield is where most games are won or lost. Take command of the midfield and you'll dominate the match. So, good midfielders are essential to all teams. They are soccer's most important all-rounders.

Essentially, they must possess the vision to read a game, have good ball control, pace, the ability to tackle, mark and distribute the ball over short and long distances. Midfielders are the play-makers, the brains, the engine room that drives a team, the vital link between defense and offense. They break up offenses by the opposing team, start offenses for their own side, close in for the kill and even shoot at goal if the opportunity presents itself.

Because midfielders do more running than any other player on the field, they need excellent fitness and stamina.

A strong tackling midfield player can usually operate in a more defensive role by winning the ball

An outstanding midfielder should be strong, determined, athletic and always looking to switch defense to offense.

and containing the opposition in the central area before driving their team forward—a good example of such a player would be the Argentinian star Javier Mascherano.

Skilled ball-playing midfielders are better equipped to break

forwards quickly with the ball to start an offense, or hold the ball until a teammate can move into position.

Midfielders must be prepared to do a great deal of unselfish running without the ball to support

Diagram A

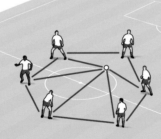
The triangle system.

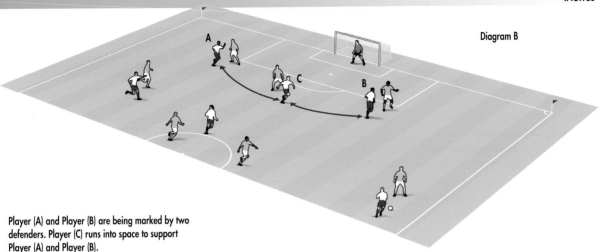

Diagram B

Player (A) and Player (B) are being marked by two defenders. Player (C) runs into space to support Player (A) and Player (B).

teammates in the last two-thirds of the field. Clever running off the ball creates space, gives teammates various options and catches opposing defenders off guard. They might be distracted by your movement long enough to allow a teammate to dribble past, move into the extra space provided or make a defense-splitting pass.

An offensive midfielder in possession of the ball often has to decide whether to hold on to it allowing teammates time to move into position, or to deliver a short,

or long pass. Passing the ball is obviously the quicker of the two options.

Long passes delivered from midfield behind defenders can launch quick offenses, bending the ball with the inside or outside of the foot around them. If you're playing against a team with a sweeper, passes out to the wings are much more effective than dribbling through the packed defense.

Most midfield play operates on the "triangle" system that allows each player at least two options

of where to pass the ball (see Diagram A).

Supporting the front-runners is an essential part of midfield play. In Diagram B the midfielder runs into space to support the two attackers who are being closely marked by defenders, giving them another option.

A long accurate pass through a crowded midfield area (see Diagram C) can often create a scoring opportunity if players are quick to spot the move and run off the ball.

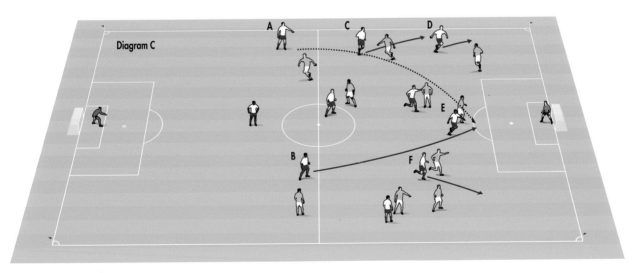

Diagram C

Player (A) passes to Player (B). The defenders are pulled out of position by attackers (C, D, E) and (F) running off the ball.

Strikers and wingers

Strikers

Goals win matches—so it's not surprising that top goalscorers are the most wanted and valued players in soccer. Brazil's Kaka and Argentina's Lionel Messi are worth their weight in goals because they have the natural ability to put the ball in the back of the net. They have an insatiable hunger for goals.

As a modern-day striker, like Spain's Fernando Torres, you need to have pace to lose a marker, the strength to hold off challenges, the ball control to retain possession and to beat an opponent. You must also have the courage to take the knocks that occur when you are being tightly marked, and the confidence to keep shooting even when the going gets tough.

But, it must be stated that good offensive play by a striker concerns more than just scoring goals. You should be able to set up chances for teammates, by acting as a target player, or a decoy, to draw defenders away from the middle of the field and create space for them to exploit.

In this role, you often receive the ball facing your own goal and should be comfortable when balls are knocked in to you from all areas of the pitch. Great strength and determination enable strikers to knock the ball down into the path of a teammate who is running into the penalty area, or six-yard box to shoot for goal. USA's Kristine Lilly is another good example.

As the target player you must make yourself available throughout the whole match, and be prepared to have a constant battle with defenders as you wait for crosses and passes from teammates.

You should always be concentrating, trying to anticipate the unexpected and be ready to seize a half-chance in front of goal.

Good strikers do not wait for chances to open up; they are continually on the move looking to play their part in offensive moves. In Diagram A, Player (A) has collected the ball on the halfway line, passes to Player (B) who passes to Player (C), who crosses for Player (A) to score after making a well-timed run.

Wingers

Wingers are usually offensive midfielders who play wide on the flanks. The old-fashioned wingers would wait for the ball to be passed to them. Recent equivalents, such as Cristiano Ronaldo of Portugal, are expected to attack, defend and even go looking for the ball if necessary.

Wingers create space on the flanks, run at fullbacks and cross the ball to their central attackers from the touchline, or move inside to shoot for goal. Crosses made

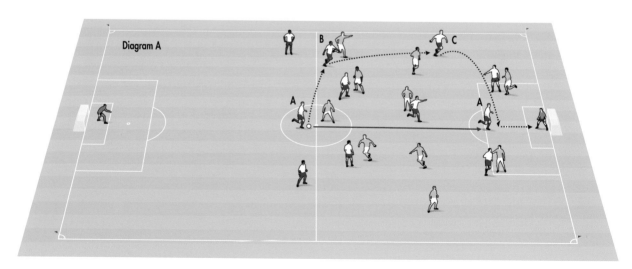

Diagram A

Player (A) starts and finishes this move. They pass to Player (B), who passes to Player (C), who crosses for Player (A) to score.

Wingers have a job at both ends of the field—attack on offense and support their teammates on defense.

the vision to know when to hold the ball up (retain possession) until support arrives, when to cross early and when to cut inside to attack the target. There is no use in a winger making a dazzling run down the flank and crossing the ball if there's nobody who can get on the end of it. Equally there is no point in running inside to the penalty area if the path to goal is crowded with players.

When a fullback makes a break down the flank, the winger should be prepared to drop back and cover that position if possession is lost. Wingers and fullbacks generally work together to create an overlap. This involves a winger in possession passing to an unmarked teammate on the flank. They then run around their marker to either receive a return pass in stride from the overlapper or act as a decoy, leaving the marker stranded. The problem with the overlap is that if an offensive player loses possession they are both left out of position (Diagram B).

from the goal line must curve away from the goal. If a defender is running back with an attacker they will find it hard to clear the ball without conceding a corner or throw-in near their line, while the goalkeeper may struggle to reach the cross.

Obviously wide players need to possess pace. They must also have

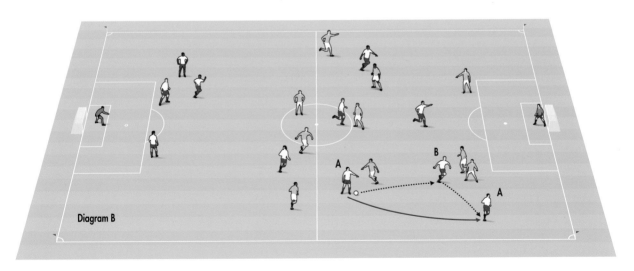

Diagram B

Player (A) passes the ball to Player (B). Player (A) then runs around their marker to take a return pass from Player (B).

Attacking strategy: switching the point of attack

Defenders are vulnerable when they are pulled out of position by opponents who suddenly switch the point of offense and get the ball into space where there is no cover.

They are also handicapped when forced to turn by an attacker who gets in behind them. A "switch movement" by an attacker can often unbalance a defender forced to turn around in order to keep the game in full view. Teams will switch the direction of play by building an offense on one side of the field, say the left. So the defense shapes to cover the left side, anticipating a break-through. In doing so, if the defense leaves a gap on the right side, an attacker should run into the space ready to take a pass from the left.

The player with the ball should then switch the point of offense with a pass across the pitch to a teammate who has just run into the open space. This movement forces the opposing defense to regroup to deal with the new situation, costing them the advantage.

But forwards are not the only players who can switch the direction of play to build an offense. The goalkeeper should be looking to throw the ball out to the wings at every opportunity. A fullback pushing forwards might get in two or three passes on their side of the pitch and then switch play with a 30-yard (27.5m) pass to a teammate on the opposite flank. Suddenly switching play in this

situation also gives the defense a chance to get back into position before losing possession.

This tactic can be particularly effective when making a direct attack on goal. In Diagram A the central striker (A) begins to move towards the right flank where teammate (C) is running, with defender (X) covering. But (A) suddenly turns and passes to their left winger (B) who is in the space created by defender (Y) moving across to cover central defender (Z) against the threat developing down the middle.

Switching the direction of offense requires good vision and an awareness of the pattern of play being used by the opposition.

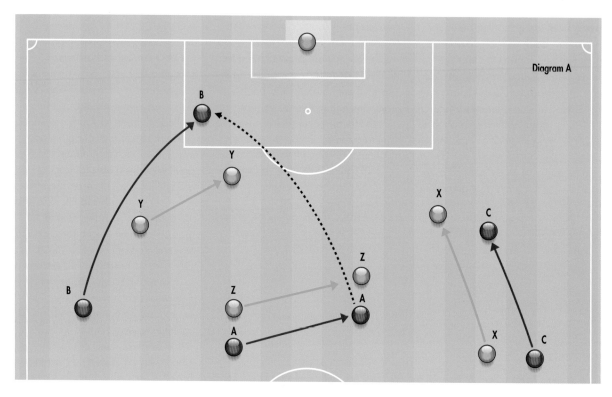

Diagram A

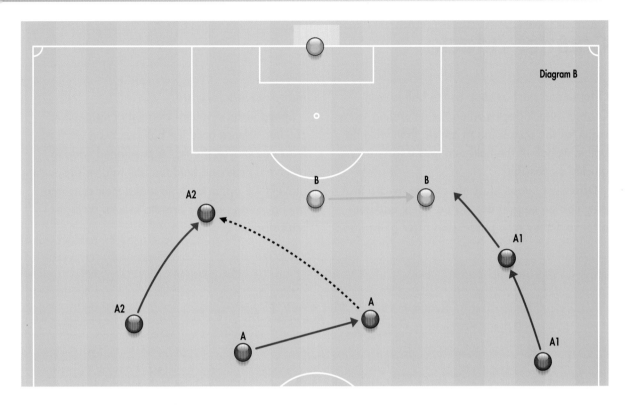

Diagram B

Pace, accuracy, anticipation and determination are obviously important. So is feinting to deceive opponents.

England's Steven Gerrard is one of the finest examples of a player with the ability to turn defense into offense with a long pass or penetrating run.

In Diagram B, offensive player (A) shapes to pass to (A1). Defender (B) moves across to cover, but (A) switches play and passes to (A2).

In Diagram C midfielder (A) has possession and two teammates (B) and (C) move into position to receive a pass. Midfielder (A) suddenly turns towards teammate (B) on their right. At the same time a second midfielder (D) runs through the gap created by offensive player (C) moving out left and takes a pass from midfielder (A) leaving them with a clear run on the goal.

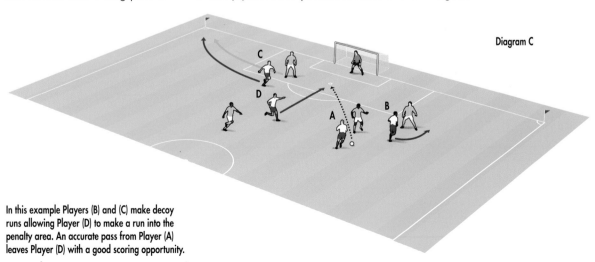

Diagram C

In this example Players (B) and (C) make decoy runs allowing Player (D) to make a run into the penalty area. An accurate pass from Player (A) leaves Player (D) with a good scoring opportunity.

Counter-attack

Offense can start as soon as the ball is won. Counter-attack begins when the defending team waits for the opposition to attack, then wins the ball in its half of the field and gets it forward as quickly as possible.

Offensive teams must always be aware that they can be caught out with a quick counter-offense if they lose possession after getting too many players forward.

Speed is the essential element of successful counter-offense once the ball has been won. At least one player should be positioned wide to receive a pass and hold the ball to give supporting players the opportunity to make their runs into the opposing penalty area to meet a cross, or return pass.

Diagram A

Player (A) passes to Player (B) who runs forwards. Player (A) runs inside and receives the ball from Player (B) to shoot.

Diagram B

Player (A) wins the ball and lofts an accurate 30-yard pass to Player (B) who is in a good position to run for goal.

Support play

Good counter-offense also depends on other members of the team playing a supporting role by pushing up to get opponents out of the half. They should also be ready to pounce on loose balls from hasty clearances or rebounds.

Defenders often make good counter-offensive players after gaining possession. In Diagram A right back (A) has won the ball and quickly passes to winger (B) and shouts "Hold it (and the player's name)!" Right back (A) then runs wide and behind the winger. When level with the winger the right back calls for the ball back and runs towards the opposition penalty area to either shoot for goal, or cross to teammate (C) who has made a good forward run.

In Diagram B defender (A) has gained possession to break up an offense, spots striker (B) in an onside position inside the opposition half and delivers a 30-yard (27m) pass to set striker (B) off on a run at goal.

Playing in the "hole"

This is a term to describe a player who plays, or pushes up into an area just behind the two main strikers (see Diagram C). The player could be a midfielder, a winger or even another striker taking up that supporting position.

Playing in the "hole" can prove an effective offensive tactic because it gives the opposition's midfield and defense a problem as to who should be marking the extra player.

It is important to inspire in all of your offensive players the confidence and ability to take on defenders in one-to-one situations. In modern soccer, defenses are so well organized that it is often the dribbling skills which can make all the difference between success or failure when sides are evenly matched.

Diagram C

Defense

Midfield

A

Attacker

Attacker

Player (A) moves forwards into the "hole" behind the two attackers.

The long-ball game

The long-ball game has a poor reputation in many people's eyes. They claim this direct style of getting the ball forward to the strikers as quickly as possible requires little skill and reduces midfield play.

But it is unfair criticism of what can be a very effective style of offensive play. The long-ball game demands a very high level of skill when used correctly, not only from the passer of the ball but also from the receiving attacker.

When making a long pass make sure the ball lands behind a defender. If the opposition is playing with a sweeper, the ball should be lofted to the wings. Against a tight defense, a long-ball pass down the center to a teammate who has made an angled run can often catch the opposition out and result in a goal being scored.

The long ball down the middle of the pitch is an excellent way of beating a well-organized offside trap, because the runner comes from deep to chase the ball. Very few defenses have the confidence to stick to their tactics when their line is breached by a player running from inside their own half.

Who does what?

There are two elements to the long pass: the passer's accuracy in finding a teammate at long range, and the skill of the receiver to control the ball and then create, or take the chance that comes from the pass.

In the late 1970s and early 1980s, France's Michel Platini was one of the world's greatest players because of his all-round soccer talent. He was probably one of the best passers of the ball ever to play for France. The fans will always remember the occasions when Michel Platini sprayed passes all over the field; more often than not finding his teammates in good open positions and setting up dangerous offenses in the process.

Platini's passing skills would have been wasted if he didn't have players around her who could do the simple things: trapping the ball, heading, turning past a defender, timing a run.

The long-ball game, if used as a part of your tactical gameplan, can be skillful and prove a very effective surprise weapon—as the diagrams on these two pages show.

The four diagrams here show how the long ball can be used as a devastating offensive weapon. Team (A), wearing the blue shirts and white shorts, are attacking from right to left. Team (B) are in red and white.

Team B's attack breaks down deep in Team A's half of the field. Team A now launch a counter-strike of devastating simplicity.

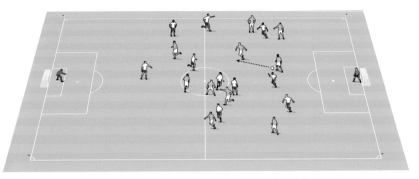

A Team A defender intercepts the ball and plays a 10-yard pass to a fellow midfielder. Team B, however, seems to have plenty of cover.

Diagram shows simplified positioning for playing in the channels.

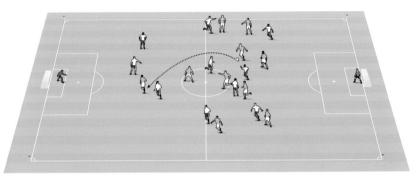

The Team A midfielder takes a few steps with the ball and then hits a beautifully weighted, right-foot pass to split the Team B defense. Danger looms.

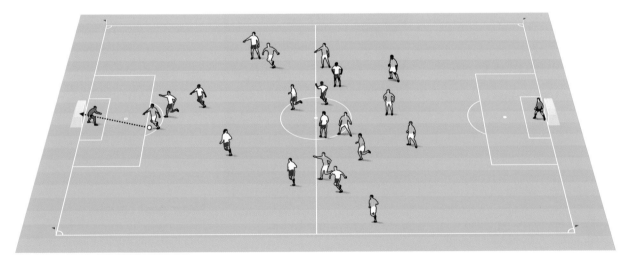

The ball lands perfectly in the path of the Team A striker, who has made a well-timed run, to deftly control the ball, and guides a shot past the Team B goalkeeper.

Playing the channels

Defenders can set up moves in their own half of the field by delivering the ball into an imaginary channel in the opposition's half (see the diagram top right). Strikers can make their moves knowing the ball will be passed into these areas. The channels are wide areas of the field, so unless the ball is hit with too much power it will not run through to the goalkeeper. If the ball is played with quality into a channel and does not run out of play, it can put the opposition under a great deal of pressure.

Set-piece play

Teams must plan and practice taking set-pieces or dead-ball kicks so that players become aware of what is expected of them when they are awarded during a game. Coaches should work on different routines to avoid being predictable. They shouldn't just concentrate on the players taking the kicks, either. The players not involved in taking free kicks also have an important job to do, like making decoy runs and moving into various positions to distract and stretch the opposition.

Free kicks, direct or indirect, can occur anywhere on the field and require adaptability and imagination if they're to be successful. Set-plays should be kept relatively simple. Involving too many players often results in confusion and a wasted opportunity.

It's best to have two, or at most three players line up to take a free kick. This keeps the opposition guessing as to which player is going to take the kick, and whether it's going to be a shot, a pass or a floated cross.

Quick free kicks

When you are taking a free kick or corner kick, it's best to cross the ball with plenty of pace. This is far harder to defend against than letting the ball "hang" in the air, and restricts the possibility of the defense rectifying a lack of concentration in its marking.

Providing the referee lets you, and your players are where the situation calls for them to be, quickly taken free kicks keep the game flowing and don't allow the opposition much time to organise a defense.

Throw-ins

A throw-in taken deep in the opposition's half of the field can be an effective offensive weapon. It should always be regarded as an opportunity to make a through pass and not merely a means of restarting play. The player taking the throw is often left unmarked and is therefore in the ideal position to receive the ball back. In this situation, throw the ball to the feet of the receiving teammate, who can more easily control and return it.

Attacking players must aim to be the first to react to set-piece opportunities for their team.

When a teammate has moved away from a marker, aim to throw the ball alongside the player so that it can be taken on the stride.

Use a long-throw player when the ball goes out of play near the opposition's penalty area. The long reach is an opportunity to

get the ball to the opposition goal's near post.

Corners

This excellent offensive opportunity can be played to wherever you feel you have the best chance to take advantage of the situation. Inform your teammates of the intended target when taking a corner kick. This information can be relayed by previously agreed hand signals (like calls in football, these should obviously be kept secret). Keep the signals simple, though. One raised arm might mean an inswinger, for instance, two raised arms an outswinger.

Near-post corner

The target is the corner of the goal area and the near post for an attacker to run in and flick the ball on at an angle, or deflect in backwards. This inswinging corner (see Diagram A) is particularly difficult to defend against because it provides the attacking team with options to alter the offense.

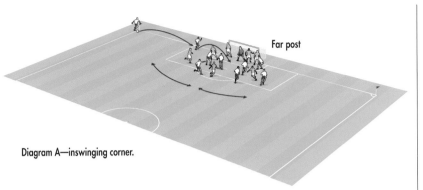

Diagram A—inswinging corner.

concentrate on the interloper rather than the kicker. An attacker in the wall can also move just as the kick is taken, making a hole for the kicker to aim at. If the shot goes through the wall, the goalkeeper may not see the ball until the last moment. Also have one or two players making dummy runs into the penalty area to confuse the opposition further.

Penalty kicks

Taking penalty kicks is all about confidence. If you are not happy about taking a penalty, don't! Placing the penalty kick needs great accuracy. Choose the spot you are aiming at and go for it—don't change your mind during the run-up. Aiming at the corner of the back of the net makes it virtually impossible for the goalkeeper to reach the ball. A little sway, or feint of the body as you run up makes it more difficult for the goalkeeper to predict which side you are aiming at.

Blasting a penalty kick relies on power and accuracy. With the longer run-up necessary, more care is needed in deciding where to put the ball. Once the run's started, keep your eyes on the ball, not the goalkeeper. Get your body over the ball and strike low, following through with the kicking leg.

Far-post corner

The basic corner kick, aimed at the far side of the penalty area and far post, is easier to defend against than the near-post variation (see Diagram B).

The cross has to be accurate over a longer distance. Defenders have more time to deal with the threat and goalkeepers see more of the ball, making it far easier to attack and collect.

It is important to position players at the near post to block the goalkeeper's view and keep defenders guessing. The kicker should curl the ball into the penalty area for a tall attacker to take the height advantage and head at goal, or knock the ball down to cause confusion, or into a teammate's path to get a shot in.

The short corner

If the kicker spots an unmarked teammate close in, there's an option to play a short pass. The receiving player can either take the ball along the goal line before crossing, pull it back outside the penalty area for a long shot at goal, or play it back to the corner taker who has run wide. Short corners can force defenders out of the penalty area, leaving gaps behind them for the offensive team to exploit.

Attacking free kicks

Any free kick awarded up to 25 yards (23m) from goal is a potential scoring opportunity for the attacking team, as defenders have to be ten yards (9m) from the ball. A free kick within shooting distance also forces the opposition to set up a defensive wall.

You can cause this defensive wall serious problems by bending the ball around it, but it's a move requiring great skill. David Beckham, the England midfielder, has scored many sensational goals from brilliant swerving free kicks. Another option is to side-foot the ball into the path of a teammate for them to shoot for goal.

When free kicks are taken, placing attackers in the opposition's wall can unsight the goalkeeper and upset the defenders—they

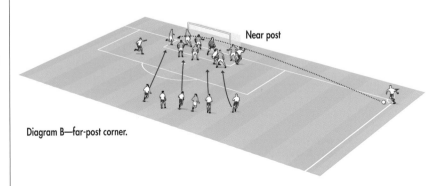

Diagram B—far-post corner.

Covering and marking

All successful teams are built on well-organized, strong defense. The main task of any defense is to stop the opposition scoring by marking attackers closely and denying them the space in which to move with the ball.

Good defending is also about winning the ball back as quickly as possible and launching a counter-offense.

In the past, defense mainly consisted of a goalkeeper, two fullbacks who marked two wingers and a big, tall center-half who controlled the central area in front of the goal.

In the modern game, defenders have to be as fast, athletic and as skilled as the forwards they are marking. To defend well you must also have good tactical awareness in order to adjust to the various conditions and strategies of the opposition.

Good defending also relies on teamwork and developing an almost telepathic understanding with your fellow defenders. You must know each other's capabilities and shortcomings; you must also be aware of your teammates' positions during a game.

Communication is another vital requirement. Defenders must talk to each other constantly. Don't be afraid to shout instructions to teammates, to warn them of challenges, tell them where and when to pass the ball. A good call in the penalty area, for example at a corner, will often prevent two defenders going for the same ball and getting in each other's way.

It is essential that defenders learn and master the art of positioning. Always ensure you are between your opponent and the ball. Restrict their space by jockeying opponents into positions where they can't be a threat, and don't allow them to get close enough so that they can easily turn you.

World-class defenders don't commit themselves in a challenge for the ball unless they are sure of winning it (or know a teammate is covering them). If you fail to win the ball in a tackle, your opponent will have your teammate to contend with and not be given a clear run.

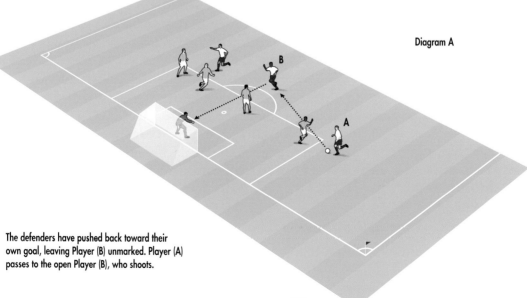

Diagram A

The defenders have pushed back toward their own goal, leaving Player (B) unmarked. Player (A) passes to the open Player (B), who shoots.

Diagram B

The defenders (A) and (B) have moved across to cover and the defense is much better balanced to deal with the situation.

Tight marking

Your actions should always be determined by the position of the ball. You should either mark your opponent closely, drop to cover a teammate, or pull away from your opponent to keep your team's shape and balance. The closer you are to the ball the more closely you should mark.

Close support

Except when you have a specific man-marking role (when you follow your opponent everywhere), you should drop off from your opponent to cover a teammate who is now moving in to mark tightly. Take up a position close enough to support your teammate, and be ready to move in and challenge if they are beaten. You should also move up and mark your designated attacker if the ball is passed to them.

Defensive balance

If the ball is at a distance and there is little opportunity for an opponent to make a long pass to the player you are marking, remain alert and be prepared to support your central defenders or provide cover for a fullback. But be aware of the player you are supposed to be marking. They may be waiting for you to move!

In Diagram A the defenders have pushed back towards their own goal, leaving an attacker unmarked and in a good position to shoot. In Diagram B, however, the defenders are more aware of the situation, having covered a possible run, and they are better balanced to deal with the attack.

Safety first

If you are challenged close to your own goal, you should not attempt to dribble the ball into safety or pass while under pressure. You should clear your lines as quickly as possible. The best way to do this is to play it into touch.

The general rule here is "play the way you are facing." It may seem a negative tactic to kick the ball into touch, or even give a corner kick away, but it is better than losing the ball in the tackle (or by having your pass intercepted) in the danger zone. Many goals are given away by defenders trying to be too clever in their own penalty area and losing possession.

One-on-one marking

One-on-one marking

There are two principal methods of defending: one-on-one and the zonal marking system. The one-on-one system (as shown in Diagram A) is self-explanatory and the most commonly used by teams.

It involves individual defenders marking one offensive player instead of space. When the opposition is in offense, defenders should know which players they are responsible for and follow them closely. When an offense starts, the defense should quickly take up position, marking one-on-one, especially those close to the ball.

This is a slightly risky strategy without a spare player, because as soon as a forward gets past a marker, the defense is outnumbered, generally leaving the offensive team with a clear run to goal. If an attacker gets through, the nearest defender should go for the tackle, leaving other defenders to cover the player left unmarked.

Ensuring adequate cover of an attacker while the player in possession is being tackled is of the utmost importance.

In Diagram B, when attacker (A) is being tackled by defender (X), defenders (Y) and (Z) are covering attackers (B) and (C).

(Y) and (Z) are positioned slightly behind (B) and (C) so they can react to any movement.

As (C) moves to (C1), (Z) also moves to (Z1) and is ready to intercept the ball or tackle (C).

If (A) dribbles past (X), the situation changes.

Three attackers (A), (B) and (C) are faced with only two defenders (Y) and (Z). If neither (Y) or (Z) leave their players to tackle (A), (A) will have a clear run to goal. But if (Y) leaves (B), then (A) can pass to (B) with little risk of interception.

The zonal system

Zonal marking is an effective alternative to one-on-one marking and is often used by British League clubs.

In Diagram C defenders are responsible for guarding their area or zone of the field and marking any attacker who comes into it. Unlike one-on-one marking, where a defender will follow their opponent

anywhere, the zonal system allows a defender to hand over responsibility to a teammate if an attacker crosses into the next zone.

Zonal marking requires good understanding between defenders, who must not be pulled out of position. They'll leave gaps if they stray too far out of their zone.

For example, a right-winger running down the flank with the ball is marked by the left-back. If the winger moves inside and across the field they get picked up by the defender in the next zone. A midfielder will, of course, need to cover the opposing winger.

Flat back four

This means having four defenders in a straight line across the back. Each player should hold position and pick up any attacker who comes into their zone. Because defenders are in a flat line they must be aware of runs from strikers and midfield players into forward areas.

If an offense comes down the right, the back four should move across in a line in that direction. The defenders should be covering each

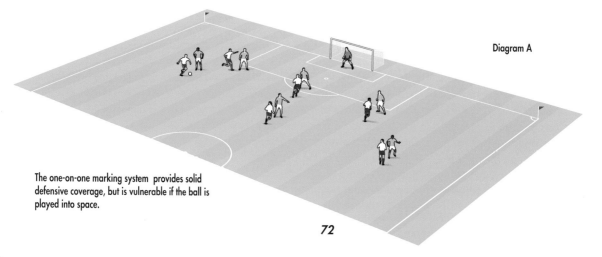

The one-on-one marking system provides solid defensive coverage, but is vulnerable if the ball is played into space.

Diagram A

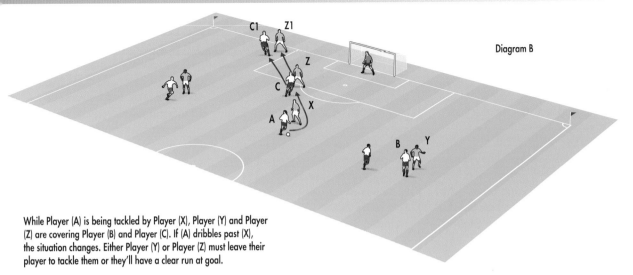

Diagram B

While Player (A) is being tackled by Player (X), Player (Y) and Player (Z) are covering Player (B) and Player (C). If (A) dribbles past (X), the situation changes. Either Player (Y) or Player (Z) must leave their player to tackle them or they'll have a clear run at goal.

other and remain aware of the lack of protection on the field's left side.

If an offense comes through the middle, the back four should move in to a pyramid formation, which forces the attackers to play the ball out wide. Good communication between the back four players is essential for the system to work well. When it is safe to move up, or to catch the opposition offside, the central defender or goalkeeper should give the order.

Those sides adopting a flat back four frequently protect them with at least one defensive central midfield player. If possession of the ball is lost during offense, the job of this player is to make sure the back four are not exposed to dangerous offenses.

Funnel defense

When a team is pressed towards its own goal, defenders should "funnel" opponents into crowded areas in the center of the pitch. Fullbacks stand on the touchline side of their opponents, forcing them to go inside where they have a better chance to intercept the ball and cover each other.

Funnel defense's advantages are: that it stops opponents getting crosses in; means central defenders are not pulled out of position; and attackers are caught offside. If the ball is played behind the back four, the goalkeeper can come out and take it. This system only works when midfielders join central defenders at the back.

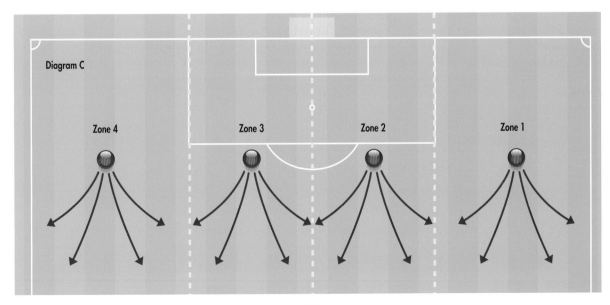

Diagram C

Zone 4   Zone 3   Zone 2   Zone 1

One-on-one marking with a sweeper

A variation on the one-on-one marking system, the defense lines up with players marking their respective opponents. A lone player is placed behind the line, with the task of rectifying any mistakes that might occur. This extra player—the sweeper—doesn't mark an attacker but acts as a safety valve to relieve offensive pressure by barring any opponent beating the defense line (Diagram A).

As soon as the sweeper has the ball the players in the defense line will need to get free of the opponents they've previously been marking. Playing behind the defense, the sweeper has an overall view of the game and is in the ideal position to intercept through-balls, start counter-offense with a long pass and even move forwards as an extra attacker. From this reorguard position, the sweeper is also best placed to signal for the offside trap to be sprung.

The offside trap

Before the ball is played, the defense moves out in a line at a given signal (see Diagram B). This often catches attackers offside, or forces them to play the ball back towards their own half of the field.

Played correctly, the offside trap can prove an effective method of breaking up offense and keeping the action as far away from your goal as possible.

Playing the offside trap requires good teamwork, communication and discipline. But teams should not use this tactic too often in a game. It frustrates the opposition and encourages attackers to take on opponents by dribbling straight through, or to beat the trap with quick passing movements. If an attacker breaks through the offside trap successfully with a carefully timed run, there is often a clear path through to goal. In fact, many goals are scored by attackers beating the offside trap.

Defensive play at set-pieces

Free kicks can be dangerous offensive weapons because they present the opposition with the opportunity of bringing extra players forward to execute carefully planned moves. But they can be defended against.

Defenses are often caught out with a variety of pre-planned moves that result in goals. Set-piece situations are a real test of defenses and their organizational abilities.

There are a number of basic rules to follow when defending free kicks. They are:
(1) In training decide on which players your team will use to form a defensive wall in matches;
(2) Concentrate on the situation because many players lose concentration when the ball goes dead;
(3) Get as many players as possible back behind the ball and switch to one-on-one marking, otherwise the defending team could find itself outnumbered;
(4) Don't get distracted by the opposition moving around and calling to teammates;
(5) Be aware of threatening blind-side runs;
(6) Leave one player free to pounce on rebounds or clearances from the defensive wall.

Diagram A

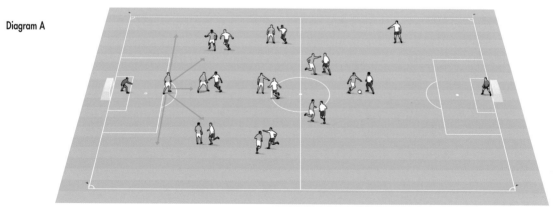

This system relies on one-on-one marking, with a sweeper playing a roving role behind the defense as a safety valve.

Diagram B

Defenders move up in a line at a given signal
before the ball is played.

Defending set-pieces

Building a wall
The "defensive wall" is built to
protect the part of the goal that
the goalkeeper might not be able
to reach, as well as attackers'
passing movements.

Defensive walls are needed when
a direct, or indirect free kick has
been awarded in a position from
which a shot can prove dangerous.

Although the goalkeeper usually
organizes the wall (to provide
a good cover from shots while
retaining as clear a view as possible
of the attackers), the keeper should
not have sole responsibility. Another
defender standing ten yards (9m)
behind the kicker should judge the
flight of the ball and direct the wall
with the aid of the goalkeeper.

It's better if your defenders
concentrate on marking opposing
attackers—or picking up central
defenders who have moved
forwards—rather than standing in
the wall. Midfielders are the best
players to have in a wall, with
the tallest standing on the outside
of the wall to block a swerving
shot. The anchor player in second

A solid, well-organized wall is crucial for
defending free kicks into the penalty box.

place should also be tall enough to counter the chip shot. This player must also ensure that the wall is not pulled out of position.

The number of players in the wall should be decided by the goalkeeper. As a rule five or six should defend a kick that has been awarded in a central position near the penalty area (two should be enough for a kick taken from an acute angle at the side of the area). If the kick is indirect inside the penalty area six to seven players should form in the wall.

- The wall should be positioned to cover one side of the goal, allowing the goalkeeper a clear view of the ball from the other side.
- Despite what you may have seen, players in the wall should not link arms because this restricts their movement. However, it is sometimes advisable to protect sensitive parts of the body with the arm or the hand.

- If you're in the wall you should be brave and not duck when the kick is taken, no matter how hard the ball has been struck.
- While staying on the right side of the laws, prevent opponents from getting into your wall. An attacker can stand less than ten yards (9m) from the kick and move away from the wall at the critical moment, leaving a gap for the free kick taker to shoot through.
- If, when the kick is taken, the ball is pushed sideways, players in the wall should not be tempted to charge out of position as a unit. The wall should remain firm, while the defender at the end of the wall nearest the ball attacks it.
- If you manage to block the free kick, you should push out as quickly as possible. This is the ideal moment to take the initiative and launch a counter-offense, while the attacking team still has the majority of its players committed to your half. Your

fullbacks should break quickly from defense, with the midfielders in support to either run with the ball or pass it accurately.

- When defending set-pieces, move quickly upfield once the kick has been cleared to deny attackers space and to catch them offside.
- Defending against free kicks taken from wide positions is much easier because a direct shot on goal is less likely. If the ball is positioned on either wing a cross will probably follow. In this situation a two-player wall should be enough to prevent a clear shot at goal.

Defending corner kicks

The goalkeeper is the key player when defending corner kicks because they can catch the cross. They should stand just inside the far post a yard off the line and shout to tell the defenders if they are going to attack the ball. In penalty areas, or for inswinging corners, the goalkeeper may prefer standing

Players can leap to block a rising free kick and protect their goal.

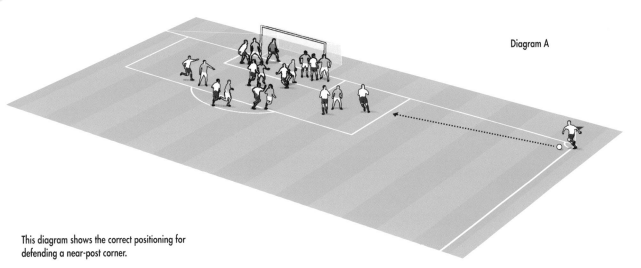

This diagram shows the correct positioning for defending a near-post corner.

halfway across the goal.

Marking should be one-on-one, or zonal with defenders positioned between their opponents and the ball but slightly in front of it to give them the space to attack the ball. A defender should be placed just inside each post, standing about a yard inside the post. From this position they can cover shots aimed at the corner of the goal and allow their goalkeeper room to attack the ball without blocking the view.

But some goalkeepers like the six-yard box clear of defenders so that they have room to go for the ball.

For balls played towards the far post at corners, defenders should stand just outside the six-yard box, one in line with the far post and the other in line with the edge of the box and others marking either attackers or zones.

Defending throw-ins

At short throw-ins the player receiving the ball will probably try to play the ball back to the thrower, so close down the receiver and mark the thrower to compromise this option.

Long throw-ins should be treated like corners and defended as such. Mark the space behind and in front of opponents likely to receive the ball and cut down space in the penalty area.

Defenders have two distinct advantages at long throw-ins: more time is taken by the thrower and it is generally clear where the ball will be delivered. Defenders are also given an opportunity to head the ball clear, since it's usually lofted high into the air towards their goal.

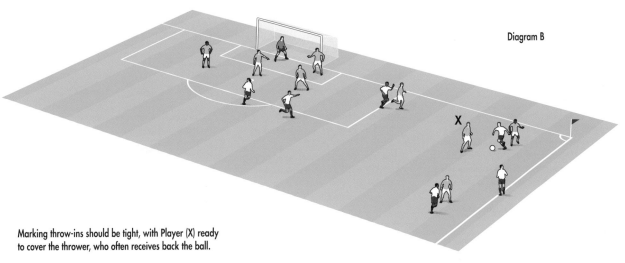

Marking throw-ins should be tight, with Player (X) ready to cover the thrower, who often receives back the ball.

GLOSSARY

Advantage: When a referee decides not to award a free kick to a team because a stoppage would mean they would lose the advantage gained.

Anchor-player: A midfield player whose main role is to win the ball.

Angle: Applied to the direction in which the ball is traveling. Goalkeepers come off their line to "narrow the angle." Attackers will drop off opponents to make a better angle for a teammate. Defenders cut down the potential scoring area by moving to cover space between the attacker and the goal.

Back four: The four back defenders who form a line of defense in front of goal.

Back-heel: Striking or passing the ball with the back (heel) of the boot.

Ball watching: Watching the ball, or going to it, and not being aware where your opponent is running to or standing.

Bicycle kick: An acrobatic overhead kick (usually a volley) made with one's back to the target.

Blind side: The opposite side of a player to the ball, or an area outside your marker's line of vision.

Block tackle: A tackle made in an upright position, with the side of the foot facing the opponent.

Booking: See Caution

Box: The penalty area.

Caution: When the referee notes a player's name (and number, if any) for a number of offenses, either persistent misconduct or unsporting conduct. After administering a caution (or booking as it is commonly known) the referee will show a yellow card.

Centerback: One or two defenders who guard the center of defense.

Channels: Areas of play on the field into which balls are played.

Chip: A pass made by a stabbing action of the kicking foot under the ball so that it gains height and not distance.

Close down: To deny an opponent space.

Committing a defender: Ensuring that an opposing defender is brought into play by moving towards them.

Corner kick: A kick awarded to the offensive team when the ball goes out of play over the goal line and was last touched by an opponent.

Covering: When the opposition is in possession, taking a position behind your teammate, or marking a player or zone, in case they are beaten.

Cross: To play the ball from a wide position into a more central position.

Cross over: When two attacking players switch positions, having run past each other to confuse the opposition.

Cushion control: When a player stops the ball so that the body acts as a cushion to take the pace off the ball and allows it to drop to the feet. This can be done with the chest, the inside of the foot, or thigh.

The D: The arc marked outside the penalty area.

Dangerous play: When players raise either foot above waist height in a way that could cause injury to an opponent's head or upper body. The referee will award an indirect free kick for this infringement.

Dead ball: When the ball is out of play, having crossed either goal line, the touchlines or when play is stopped by the referee for a foul.

Decoy run: When an attacker makes a run to take a defender out of position with the aim of creating space for a teammate.

Defender: A player whose main role is to prevent the opposition from scoring.

Deflecting: Changing the direction of the ball without stopping it.

Diagonal run: When players run at an angle either from the wing towards goal or from the middle towards the corner.

Dribbling: A player using ball control to take the ball past several opponents.

Dropped ball: When the referee, having stopped the game while the ball was still in play, restarts the game by dropping the ball between two opposing players. Players can touch the ball as soon as it touches the ground.

Dummy: When a player feints to move in one direction and then moves away in another.

Extra time: A spell of extra play, usually 15 minutes each way, to decide a knockout game when the scores are level at the end of the normal 90-minute period.

Far post: The goal post furthest from where the ball is crossed.

Feint: See Dummy

Flank: See Wings

Flight: The trajectory of the ball.

Forward: An attacking player mainly concerned with creating and scoring goals. Also known as a striker.

Free kick (Direct): A free kick from which a goal can be scored without another player having touched the ball.

Free kick (Indirect): A free kick from which the ball must be touched by another player before a goal can be scored.

Fullback: A defender operating on either the right or left side of defense.

Goal area (or six-yard box): The 6yd x 20yd (5.5m x 18.2m) area directly in front of the goal from where goal kicks are taken.

Goal kick: A kick awarded to the defending team when the ball goes over the goal line (but not in the goal) and was last touched by an opponent.

Goal side: A defensive position where you go so that you are between an attacker and your goal.

Half-volley: When the ball is kicked just after it has made contact with the ground.

Hold: Retain possession of the ball.

Hustle: To put opponents under pressure when they have the ball.

Injury time: Time added on by the referee to the end of each half to compensate for time lost when players were receiving treatment on the field, or when play stops. Injury time is decided by the referee.

Instep: The upper surface of the foot or cleat by the big toe.

Jockeying: When a defender retreats between an attacker and the goal forcing them to go in one particular direction while other defenders move in to cover.

Libero: The European name for a sweeper (see Sweeper).

Midfield player: A player who is neither an attacker nor a defender, but links with and helps out both.

Narrowing the angle: When a goalkeeper advances towards an offensive player to cut down the amount of goal the attacker has to shoot at.

Near post: The post nearest to where the ball is crossed.

Obstruction: The act of unlawfully obstructing another player.

Offside: When an attacker has fewer than two defenders in front of them and the ball is passed forward to them.

One-on-one marking: When players exclusively mark one opponent.

One touch: Passing the ball first time to a teammate without controlling it first.

One-two: See Wall pass

Overlap: When a player runs ahead and outside of a teammate in possession to offer space for a pass.

Own goal: When a goal is scored after last being touched by a member of the defending team.

Penalty area (18-yard box): The area in which a goalkeeper can handle the ball. If a defender commits an offense in this area that is punishable by a direct free kick a penalty kick is awarded.

Penalty kick: A direct kick at goal taken 12 yards (11m) from the goal's center. While it's being taken, all players except the goalkeeper and penalty taker must be outside the penalty area and the D.

Push pass: A pass made with the inside of the foot.

Run with the ball: When a player runs with the ball at their feet.

Running off the ball: When a player makes a run to support a teammate who has the ball.

Sending off: Players sent from the Field of Play by the referee after committing serious foul play, violent conduct, foul or abusive language, or persistent misconduct after a caution in the same match. To signal that a player is being sent off the referee shows the red card.

Set play: Any pre-planned move to restart play from a free kick, corner kick or throw-in.

Shielding the ball: Placing your body in such a way as to prevent an opponent seeing or playing the ball. This is not the same as Obstruction, however.

Striker: An offensive player whose main role is to score goals.

Supporting player: A player in a position to receive a pass from a teammate in possession.

Sweeper: A defender who plays behind the other defenders, covering them and tidying up any defensive errors. Also ideally positioned to launch counter-offense.

Tackle: When a player makes a challenge and dispossesses an opposing player or wins the ball with legal use of the feet.

Through-ball: A pass through the opposing defense for a teammate to chase.

Throw-in: Restarting play after the ball has gone over the touchline. The throw has to be taken by a member of the team that did not touch the ball last.

Touchline: The longer boundary line of the Field of Play.

Turning the opponent: Forcing an opponent to turn by playing the ball past them.

Two touch: Passing the ball to a teammate after controlling it first.

Vision: A player's ability to see where other players are positioned and to understand the full range of passing options available.

Volley: Striking the ball while it's still in the air.

Wall: A barrier formed by players to block a free kick near their goal.

Wall pass: Also known as the "one-two." A quick pass is made to a teammate who immediately returns the ball to you. This is similar to kicking a ball at a wall and then playing the rebound.

Winger: A player who plays on the far left or right of the offense.

Wings: The areas of the field near the touchline.

INDEX